# Your Guide to
# CORSICA

by

## GEOFFREY WAGNER

## ALVIN REDMAN
### LONDON

First Published by
ALVIN REDMAN LIMITED
107 Jermyn Street, St. James's, London, S.W.1
1 9 6 0

Printed in Great Britain by
CRUSHA & SON, LTD.,
LONDON, N.17

# CONTENTS

| | PAGE |
|---|---|
| Preface by Count Peraldi .. .. .. .. .. | 11 |
| Map of Ajaccio .. .. .. .. .. .. .. | 14 |
| Map of Bastia .. .. .. .. .. .. .. | 15 |
| INTRODUCTION .. .. .. .. .. .. | 17 |
| PART ONE—THE GENERAL PICTURE .. .. .. | 21 |
| What Is Corsica? .. .. .. .. .. .. .. | 23 |

Transportation—

1. To the Island:
   - (a) By Land .. .. .. .. .. .. — 26
   - (b) By Sea:
     - (i) From France .. .. .. .. — 28
     - (ii) From Italy .. .. .. .. — 31
   - (c) By Air:
     - (i) From England .. .. .. .. — 32
     - (ii) From France .. .. .. .. — 32

2. On the Island:
   - (a) By Land:
     - (i) By Car .. .. .. .. .. — 35
     - (ii) By Train .. .. .. .. .. — 38
     - (iii) By Bus .. .. .. .. .. — 39
   - (b) By Sea .. .. .. .. .. .. — 40

| Passport—Identification .. .. .. .. .. .. | 41 |
| Currency—Traveller's Cheques .. .. .. .. .. | 42 |
| Insurance .. .. .. .. .. .. .. .. | 46 |
| History .. .. .. .. .. .. .. .. | 46 |
| Language .. .. .. .. .. .. .. .. | 61 |
| People .. .. .. .. .. .. .. .. | 65 |
| Hotels .. .. .. .. .. .. .. .. | 67 |

Motoring:
- (i) In General .. .. .. .. .. — 73
- (ii) Spares and Service Facilities .. .. .. — 74
- (iii) Petrol .. .. .. .. .. .. — 77
- (iv) Documents .. .. .. .. .. — 78
- (v) Map .. .. .. .. .. .. — 79
- (vi) Roads .. .. .. .. .. .. — 80

5

|  |  | PAGE |
|---|---|---|
| Climate | .. .. .. .. .. .. .. | 85 |
| Clothing | .. .. .. .. .. .. .. | 87 |
| Winter Sports | .. .. .. .. .. .. | 90 |
| Yachting | .. .. .. .. .. .. .. | 91 |
| "Le Camping" | .. .. .. .. .. .. | 91 |
| Beaches—Bathing and Swimming | .. .. | 99 |
| Fishing | .. .. .. .. .. .. .. | 100 |
| Food and Drink | .. .. .. .. .. | 101 |
| Tipping | .. .. .. .. .. .. .. | 110 |
| Shopping | .. .. .. .. .. .. .. | 114 |
| Taxis | .. .. .. .. .. .. .. | 117 |
| Electricity | .. .. .. .. .. .. | 118 |
| Sickness | .. .. .. .. .. .. .. | 119 |
| | | |
| PART TWO—ROUND THE COAST | .. .. .. | 121 |
| Ajaccio | .. .. .. .. .. .. | 124 |
| From Ajaccio to Cargèse | .. .. .. .. | 134 |
| Cargèse | .. .. .. .. .. .. | 136 |
| From Cargèse to Piana | .. .. .. .. | 137 |
| Piana | .. .. .. .. .. .. | 139 |
| From Piana to Porto | .. .. .. .. | 142 |
| Porto | .. .. .. .. .. .. | 144 |
| From Porto to Calvi | .. .. .. .. | 145 |
| Calvi .. | .. .. .. .. .. | 146 |
| From Calvi to Ile Rousse | .. .. .. | 151 |
| Ile Rousse | .. .. .. .. .. | 153 |
| From Ile Rousse to Saint-Florent | .. .. | 154 |
| Saint-Florent | .. .. .. .. .. | 156 |
| Cap Corse | .. .. .. .. .. | 158 |
| Bastia | .. .. .. .. .. .. | 162 |
| From Bastia to Solenzara | .. .. .. | 168 |
| Solenzara | .. .. .. .. .. .. | 171 |
| From Solenzara to Porto-Vecchio | .. .. | 172 |
| Porto-Vecchio | .. .. .. .. .. | 173 |
| From Porto-Vecchio to Bonifacio | .. .. | 177 |
| Bonifacio | .. .. .. .. .. | 178 |
| From Bonifacio to Propriano | .. .. | 181 |
| Propriano | .. .. .. .. .. | 183 |
| From Propriano to Ajaccio | .. .. .. | 188 |
| | | |
| PART THREE—INTO THE INTERIOR | .. .. | 191 |
| *Ajaccio—Vizzavona—Corte—Bastia* | .. .. | 193 |
| Vizzavona | .. .. .. .. .. | 195 |
| Corte | .. .. .. .. .. .. | 197 |
| *Porto—Evisa—Calacuccia—Le Niolo—Asco—La Balagne* | .. | 200 |
| Evisa | .. .. .. .. .. .. | 202 |
| Calacuccia | .. .. .. .. .. | 203 |

|  |  | PAGE |
|---|---|---|
| Asco | .. .. .. .. .. .. .. .. | 205 |
| *Solenzara—Zonza—Porto-Vecchio* | .. .. .. .. | 207 |
| Zonza | .. .. .. .. .. .. .. .. | 209 |
| *Ghisoni—Zicavo—Sartène* .. | .. .. .. .. .. | 210 |
| Sartène | .. .. .. .. .. .. .. .. | 211 |

PART THREE—CHARTS AND APPENDICES .. .. 215

Itineraries:
| | |
|---|---|
| (1) A Two-Week Itinerary by Car .. .. .. .. | 217 |
| (2) An Eight-Day Itinerary by Car or Bus .. .. .. | 218 |
| (3) A Seven-Day Tour of Corsica via Europabus (No. 532) | 219 |

Conversion Tables—
| | |
|---|---|
| (1) Measures of Length .. .. .. .. | 219 |
| (2) Measures of Weight .. .. .. | 220 |
| (3) Measures of Capacity .. .. .. | 220 |
| (4) Time Changes .. .. .. .. | 220 |
| (5) Clothing Sizes .. .. .. .. | 221 |
| (6) Tyre Pressures .. .. .. .. | 221 |
| (7) Fahrenheit and Centigrade .. .. | 221 |
| (8) Film Ratings .. .. .. .. | 222 |
| (9) Currency Conversion .. .. .. | 222 |

Glossaries—
| | |
|---|---|
| (1) Cooking Terms .. .. .. .. .. | 222 |
| (2) Motoring Terms .. .. .. .. .. | 224 |
| (3) Road Signs .. .. .. .. .. | 225 |

| | |
|---|---|
| Postal Rates .. .. .. .. .. .. .. | 225 |
| Scales of Self-Drive Car Hire .. .. .. .. .. | 226 |
| A Brief Chronology of Corsica .. .. .. .. .. | 226 |
| A Select Bibliography of Books in English on Corsica, written during this century .. .. .. .. .. .. | 227 |

INDEX .. .. .. .. .. .. .. .. 229

# ILLUSTRATIONS

1. Ajaccio: from the Bois des Anglais.
2. Ajaccio harbour.
3. The Château de la Punta (extreme right) near Ajaccio.
4. Typical Calanches near Piana.
5. Cargèse: showing the two churches, Greek and Roman Catholic, which dominate the village.
6. Coming down to Porto from Piana.
7. Porto: the Marine and the peaks of Poglia-Orba.
8. The Gulf of Girolata.
9. Calvi harbour.
10. Calvi: a typical Corsican street scene.
11. Calvi: the church of Sainte-Marie-Majeure.
12. Calvi: the Citadelle.
13. Montemaggiore: a typical terraced hill village in the Balagne behind Calvi.
14. Saint-Florent: the fishermen's harbour.
15. The Convent of Pino.
16. Erbalunga: looking south down the coast of Cap Corse; Bastia can be seen in the distance.
17. Bastia: the Citadelle, dominating the entrance to the New Port
18. Bastia: a typical street scene in the Old Town.
19. Bastia harbour.
20. Porto-Vecchio: the author on the Palombaggia plage.
21. Porto-Vecchio: the Palombaggia plage.
22. Bonifacio: the Marine.
23. The inlet under Porto-Vecchio.
24. Bonifacio: the cliff on which the Haute Ville stands.
25. Corte: Place de l'Eglise.
26. Monte d'Oro: landscape typical of the Vizzavona area.
27. The Spelunca Gorge near Evisa.
28. Evisa: looking towards the Gulf of Porto.
29. Sartène.

# ACKNOWLEDGMENT

This guide could not have been written without the generous co-operation of a number of individuals and organizations. Of these my debt is inevitably deepest to the Comte Peraldi, Président de l'ESSITAC, or the Syndicat d'Initiative Régional d'Ajaccio et de La Corse. Beyond the unwearying assistance he and his office gave me I need to thank a number of friends from Air France, the French National Railroad (SNCF), and the French Government Tourist Office, without whose aid I could have done very little. Mlle. J. Barget of the last-mentioned organization helped me enormously by opening files on Corsica to me. M. Jean Leandri, of the Association Corse, answered a number of questions for me with sympathetic enthusiasm, while George Helberg and Dick Carlson of the Columbia Travel Service uncomplainingly gave their time on my behalf over and over again. Vic Raeburn, P.R.O. of Air France, and Ron Stieglitz, Manager of Hertz International Ltd., were especially courteous and generous in their assistance to me. To all these, and the many others who helped me in Corsica itself, my warmest thanks.

# CORSICA

Is there any country in the world that has a greater claim than Corsica to the name Island of Beauty? I think not; indeed at every step, at every moment of the day it provides us with happy, moving or dramatic experiences.

Here an African village; there a French landscape; here the charms of the Riviera and there, suddenly, deep sombre gorges, like a vision in Dante!

Everywhere, or almost everywhere, in harmonious juxtaposition, are the Sea, the Mountain and the Forest, bathed in brilliant light.

Corsica is the perfect country for tourists with its thousand kilometres of coastline, of which three quarters are unbelievably varied and picturesque. It has four hundred kilometres of breathtaking railways and more than four thousand kilometres of roads. Their amazing evolutions through the vast *maquis* have been made necessary by the mountainous nature of the land and each turning reveals a different view.

Corsica is a tourist country. So be it! but the country that our English friends have so charmingly christened "The Scented Isle" is also a country for the discerning, a chosen land, a place for long enthusiastic visits, because it is one of the few remaining parts of Europe where one can find virgin nature unfolding without restraint.

To this wild natural beauty is joined a spirited race of men, one of the finest in the world, which has produced Pope Formose for the Church, Don Juan and Christopher Columbus for Spain, Colonel Général Sampiero (worth 6,000 men), two emperors and numerous maréchals for France, kings for Europe and more recently, generals, prefects, members of the government and even — several beauty queens!

Her men are worthy, her women virtuous; they are faithful and passionate. The following advice has become proverbial: "If you are going into danger take a Corsican man as your friend and if you are looking for happiness take a Corsican woman as your wife!"

It has been said of Corsica that hardly any other country in the world has such a concentration of beauty, and, one might add, of such an unusual quality. In this remarkable country the horses have the temperament of pretty women; they are as nervous as gazelles and as patient as camels. The wonderfully sure-footed mules are as fine as those the cardinals had in the sixteenth century. The wild goats are called *mouflons;* the domestic goats have the airs of film stars and an inordinate love of heights, from which they eye you solemnly with sprigs of wild laburnum hanging from their thieving mouths.

Seekers after local colour can make enthusiastic discovery of towns and villages several centuries old but unchanged in appearance and can sample the exquisite peasant hospitality, taste the perfumed "lonzo," the delectable "brocchio." Blackbirds stuffed with juniper berries or the star-shaped seeds of the mastic-tree, crayfish from the Sanguinaires Islands, trout from the mountain streams, all accompanied by local wines, appear on the tables of the most exacting gourmets.

12

And this Island of Beauty deserves also the name "Island of Health," for the whole of nature conspires to strengthen and cure the frail human body. In the first place, in an area no bigger than a French département, there is an amazing variety of climate; on the coast an average winter temperature higher than that of the Côte d'Azur is tempered in the summer by the sea breezes; only forty kilometres away are high altitude resorts in forests of beeches, pines and chestnut trees; there, almost on the threshold of sun-scorched Africa stretches "the depth of woods and their immense silence," scarcely disturbed by the splashing of waterfalls and springs that are "purer than crystal."

The air is rich in oxygen and so clear and dry that the outline of the horizon stands out with the clarity of a Greek landscape.

But the bounties of nature in Corsica are not confined to the influence of the climate. Hidden in its valleys are mineral springs with wonderful curative properties as yet still neglected or very little exploited.

Like mainland France, of which it is one of the most precious jewels, Corsica is still at the gates of war and to ask that it should show its true face in the present circumstances is a challenge, but Corsican hospitality is not an empty phrase: it is up to you to try it: Corsica awaits you.

COUNT PERALDI.

13

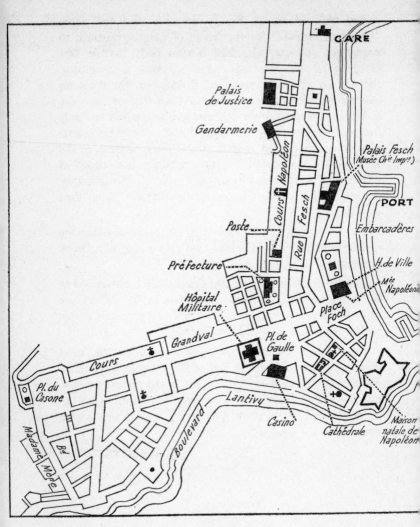

AJACCIO

14

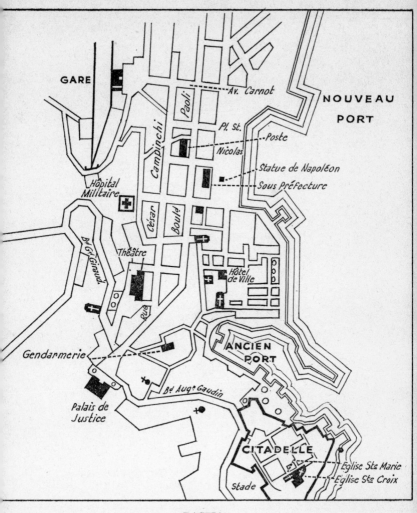

BASTIA

15

*Corsica, tanti paesi, tante usanze*

# INTRODUCTION

"One has to be dull in any comprehensive guide book," writes Mr. Cyril Connolly, reviewing (not for the first time) a book on French cooking in a recent issue of the *Sunday Times*. And if he says so, it must be true. But if this book is dull, the fault is mine, not that of Corsica.

There are, of course, two Corsicas. Perhaps three. Perhaps, rather, one should say that there are thousands — a new island for each visitor who goes there and drinks of its inexhaustible beauty for the first time.

Primarily there is Corsica itself, *"l'âme corse,"* with its sense of history, and social isolation, and deep aristocratic pride. This Corsica is only to be discovered after many years, and chiefly in the interior. Possibly it is not open to the outsider at all.

The other Corsica is the resort, one of the last grand beauty spots of Europe left in front of that continually advancing tide of our masses, and the rape of the machine. The third Corsica I tentatively referred to would be the indigenous life of the new commercial classes there today.

But in the second sense, with that silence and simplicity most of Europe left behind over a century ago, Corsica offers an unparalleled place to spend one's annual holiday. The variety of its scenery within such a short land span is extraordinary and cannot be summed up in a few sentences. Suffice it to say that from the moment the first of those old Genoese towers comes into view, presiding over some legendary, faultless reach of sand, the visitor's eye is fairly feasted with scenery.

It is to this second Corsica that most of the readers of this book will naturally go. To a brilliant sun in an azure sky, to white beaches, and to seas of Tyrian purple and limpid green, surely the clearest waters in the world.

For this reason YOUR GUIDE TO CORSICA principally emphasizes the island as a holiday resort, a refuge from our English rain, a repose of beaches and noondays shadowy with indigo-washed rocks. However, the author is the first to know that Corsica is much more than this. My attempt has been to try to include as much of the "dark" Corsica, of the interior and of the soul, as will be practically interesting to the average English traveller there. Aesthetically, of course, the first Corsica comes first. But few of us, alas, have time or opportunity to savour it these hurried, harried days. Accordingly, this guide is mainly aimed at giving useful facts for the holidaymaker, the explorer of the coastal area, the fugitive from "the worst summer on record;" ethnographic and other information is necessarily secondary.

Granted this, I should like to add that I have everywhere tried to write as honestly as possible. It does not seem to me of the slightest service to my readers to describe everything and everywhere in superlatives, in the manner of many travel-books. I have by this time met too many of my fellow-countrymen on their generally hard-earned and briefly-snatched summer holidays in Europe to have any delusions about their desires. The majority of us, and especially the young, leave England for the Mediterranean in search of natural beauty, grace of life, good food, the sea, and, above all, plenty of back-breaking sun! Needless to say, all these, and much more, may be found in Corsica. But because I believe I know what the average British traveller is looking for, I have nowhere tried to "write up" the island. Corsica simply doesn't need it. I have given warnings where I think warnings due. The comprehensive, or encyclopaedic, guide-book is not — cannot hope to be — relative, and as a result usually errs this side of idolatry.

By this I mean that a glance through one or two of the celebrated French guides will reveal almost no place that is not spoken of with enthusiasm, nay adulation. In such guides the informational detail is unsurpassed, but the brief holiday tourist finds himself at sea, confronted by such *embarras de richesses* wherein the rule that comparisons are odious has been all too closely followed.

So I have tried my best to be frank, as well as glowing, in these pages. After a while the reader should be able to come to feel the kind of yardstick I am applying to the various places visited and, even if he disagrees with my viewpoint (or aspects of it), he will at least find that it serves as a basis of comparison. The single outlook on a relatively small area does have that advantage, in any case.

Corsica is still the least spoilt and most naturally beautiful Mediterranean resort I know. How long it will remain so I do not know, but it is certainly unlikely that the machine will ever be able to corrupt the beauty of its mountain scenery, at any rate. Meanwhile, from the Côte d'Azur, where, all summer long, cars full of people looking like Françoise Sagan crawl bumper to bumper in an endless procession from St. Tropez to the Italian frontier, a daily air service takes you in an hour (or a nightly boat service in nine) from Nice to Bastia, from the world of Françoise Sagan to a purity of atmosphere that is a tonic in itself, from petrol fumes and gritty beaches to the pungent perfume of the Corsican maquis as you emerge from the silken froufrou of its waters.

Perhaps I wax rhapsodic. Very well then, put aside this book and go and buy a gramophone record, a ten-inch

French Vega long-play called *Evocation de la Corse, par ses Chants traditionnels et modernes* (F 35 M 3001); if you cannot get this, try to get hold of the twelve-inch Angel *Songs of Corsica,* sung by Martha Angelica, herself a Corsican. Although Mlle. Angelica is a perfect interpreter of these songs (some of which are duplicated on the Vega), I prefer the former disc since it is a live recording and less rehearsed in effect (1). As I write I am listening to it now, particularly the hymn *Dio Vi Salvi Regina,* the national anthem of 1735 dedicating Corsica to the Virgin Mary, which you should try to hear sung at Corte, the ancient capital, during one of the August or September festivals there. While the choir sings, the bells of the remote Corte church ring slowly in the background and, believe me, there are no bells like Corsican bells heard in the pellucid silence of a country evening there. They are like very faint pulse-beats of the past, mild twangs on some immemorial harpstring.

If you listen to this record a few times, it will tell you much about Corsica, about its sadness, its poetry and poverty, its unwillingness or inability to move with the times, its pride and its beauty. Then, put the record aside and next listen to it when you return from your trip. Even if you have only had the chance to hear some harvester in the fields, or guitarist in a café, singing with that characteristic sob in the voice, you will still hear this record differently. Immutably Corsica will have changed you. The first Corsica, in fact, will have stolen into and subtly blended with the second. You will never forget it.

(1) It is not possible to keep up with all these new folk-lore releases. Two more anthologies or medlies of Corsican folk songs have been waxed since writing the above, including *This is Corsica* sung by the excellent Toni Rocca to guitars under the Bruno label (BR 50026), while Westminster has just issued the French Vega (West. 12007).

# PART ONE

# THE GENERAL PICTURE

# WHAT IS CORSICA ?

Situated due north of Sardinia, and 98 miles south of Genoa, Corsica is the navel of the northern Mediterranean. By modern standards it is very close to both France and Italy, the distance from Marseille to Ajaccio, for instance, being only 178 sea miles and from Nice to Calvi only 95. Comprising in all a land area of 3,378 square miles, and being 114 miles long by 52 broad, Corsica ranks as the third largest island in the Mediterranean after Sicily and Sardinia. Today its population has sunk to about a quarter of a million. This "island of beauty," or "scented isle," as it is variously dubbed, was the last department to join the French commonwealth.

Such are the chief facts. What do they say of the country itself? Nothing. How, after all, can one briefly summarize an island which is no less than a universe in itself? Perhaps the visitor will be greeted by some sweet sands, by crab-coloured rocks outlined on any inky sea. He imagines he is in for a Riviera landscape. But this blessed isle can boast Alpine villages within fifty miles of such coastlines, Dutch swamps and Norman flats on the east, not to mention elsewhere Swiss waterfalls, Italian vineyards, Norwegian pines, one Asiatic desert, several Pyrenean valleys, an Engadine of its own, and a Spanish gravamen in the interior — in fact, an abstract of most of the more interesting aspects of Europe. For above all must one beware of judging this pearl of a place by its rather *arriviste* exterior. It is in those philosophic villages in the mountains that one finds the familial heritage of Greek and Roman, of Arab as well as Italian and French, within the Corsican mentality that so justly matches the enormous variety of its views. In the interior, too, among glittering cascades, one sees those transverse mountain chains which are the glory of the island and chiefly distinguish it, topographically speaking, from its neighbours. These mountains drive into labyrinths of peaks, rising sometimes to 9,000 feet and, on the eastern seaboard, descending to alluvial plains, flecked with lagoons, where palm-trees Pacifically idle.

Despite these many mountains, whose porphyry flanks haunt one's vision everywhere there, over 43 per cent. of Corsica is statistically returned as arable land. The isle is rich in wine, olives, cheeses, and pasturage for cows, goat and boar. These last you will encounter in a semi-wild state, munching and rooting amid the lush chestnut-forests. Almost everywhere there are superb olive trees, oranges, citrons, laurels, and vines.

In addition, the Corsican horizon is constantly softened by the celebrated *maquis,* which covers, in one way or another, the major part of the island. This *maquis* (or *macchia*) is a confused thicket of heather-like underbrush, varying in growth from knee to head-height, consisting in the main of cystus, myrtle, juniper, lavender, rosemary, mint, pink and white heath, honeysuckle, and so forth. This shaggy beard of the earth, so to speak, played over by Burgundy-coloured butterflies, emits a pungent perfume, a rough scent of a resinous texture not unreminiscent at times of incense. The blurred mauve of the *maquis* converts the whole island into a garden really, and legend has it that Napoleon, in exile in St. Helena, used to say that he could recognize his homeland with his eyes shut,

24

by its smell alone. This fairly touching anecdote should not be taken too literally, however. The Corsican *maquis* smells no more fervently, to my uneducated nostrils, than the same growth on certain of the Italian islands. However, the ferny bramble is certainly much thicker on Corsica and the expression *prendre le maquis,* from which the French underground took its name in the last war, is thoroughly dramatized here.

Through this countryside goat-tracks continually ramble, up towards collections of houses — villages, if you will — full of pigs and donkeys and plants in pots. Around the village pump will be grouped a few old men in velveteen trousers and coloured cummerbunds worn utterly naturally, without the slightest affectation. In fact, these decorative garments are utilitarian, they are worn for warmth in the chill mountain evenings. There is an unusual vigour apparent in these inland people, the anxious gravity of whose attentive, sensitive faces reveals more than anything the Corsican legacy of long years of poverty and oppression. And as one listens to the rough Tuscan intonation of their brogue under some melancholy tree, one realizes suddenly how much is poured into this country of both French and Italian genius, and of how the old code of Roman law still persists in the peasant family here.

One senses things like this as the animation of the open-air life of the day subsides at evening, *all'imbrunir della notte* as Paoli called his favourite time of day, Corsican twilight when the perfumed air becomes lit by glow-worms, and mandolin and guitar are heard and the houses of grey hatched into distant hillsides turn into burning jewels laid on lazy velvet.

Island and inhabitants, then, are marked by history and both possess the inherent ancestral dignity of those hard-earned scars. Tourism itself has really only just started in Corsica. In 1957 the French Government embarked on a programme of development to build one hundred hotels, with some three thousand rooms, in the island. This is a development which I, for one, have watched with gloom, I confess, although it may considerably assist the country's economy. Fortunately the Corsican *Syndicat d'Initiative* is in the hands of an aristocrat of taste and discrimination, but even so — will all the worst features of twentieth-century modernization spoil this poor, proud country? On the whole one can take strength from history in answer to this question. Corsica has resisted so many invasions in the past that it will repel the new barbarians of our own age.

The Sphinx of Corsica is said to be symbolized by the Lion of Roccapina, a strangely shaped rock of rose granite near a Genoese tower in the south. Silhouetted against that sacred sea beloved of Byron, this lion always looks to me ridden by the goddess of eternity. Ferrandi, in his *La Renaissance de la Corse,* refers to it as a natural synonym of liberty in the face of foreign despotism. I have a feeling it will still be there when the last H-bomb has dropped.

## TRANSPORTATION

### 1. TO THE ISLAND

(a) *By Land:*

This book does not aim to be a guide as to how to get across France. Michelin does that very nicely for anyone who is interested. And sometimes, driving behind the GB plates down N7 south of Lyons, I have wondered if the English any longer need routing to the Riviera. From June on all the motor traffic in France seems to head there instinctively, like a horse making for home.

Moreover, it may well be that many motorists using these pages for information will be in France already, tooling around the *côte d'Azur*, admiring the Bikini atolls. The latter lucky people need only make for one of the French ports listed in my next sub-section. Those who aim to take their own cars to Corsica across the French mainland will in any case want to form their own routes, if they are the independent Britons I think they are; and may I recommend them to get off the bursting *routes nationales* and try the secondary roads, marked yellow by Michelin, on either side of the Rhône. But even if you don't want to prowl around here and there in France and merely aim to hare south down N7, my advice would come a poor second to that of the A.A. whose *Comprehensive Overseas Touring Service* provides pretty well everything, from the Tourist Docket that has now replaced the *carnet de passage en douanes* for motorists down to the relevant maps. The whole thing only costs £3 for the A.A. member.

One local point, however: cars are carried by all the steamship services from France to Corsica listed below. I quote rates. In the season car space is fought for tooth and nail on these ships and the last time I took mine over from Marseille I had to make a June reservation in the previous January. The car has to be on the jetty six hours before departure time, doors unlocked, petrol out, and battery unhooked. Insurance is obligatory. Third party insurance is not in France, but obviously this is something one must be most careful about. See that your policy covers

27

you thoroughly and carry the green International Insurance Certificate. The Tourist Docket, by the way, must be franked on both leaves by French Customs and worn thereafter on the windscreen.

(b) *By Sea:*

(i) From France:

As explained, then, this — plus the Italian boat service — is the only way of taking your car, if you are thinking of doing so. It is also, of course, a very pleasant way of escaping the throngs on the Riviera at any time.

The three ports in France that service the island are Marseille, Nice, and Toulon; ports in Corsica that receive and send out passenger shipping include Ajaccio, Bastia, Propriano, Calvi, and Ile Rousse (sometimes spelt, on and off the island, with a definite article). During the season sailings from France are about every other day, with two ships leaving on certain dates. Marseille is 209 sea miles from Bastia, and 178 from Ajaccio; Nice is 95 from Calvi, 123 from Bastia, and 130 from Ajaccio.

This shipping is run by the Compagnie Générale Transatlantique, sometimes known as the French Line, the same that sends those floating hotels, the *Liberté* and the *Flandre* across the Atlantic. On cold paper there is actually no such company as the French Line, even though you will see these words painted on the sides of C.G.T. vessels. Because of its high percentage of Anglo-Saxon patronage the company has simply adopted the moniker on the Atlantic runs. The point I am making is — you are in good hands.

Here is the 1960 schedule of sailings from France to Corsica; to avoid confusion I have used the Army system of time, or the so-called cockeyed clock:

| Dep.      |           | Arr.    | Arr.   |
| Marseille |           | Ajaccio | Bastia |
| 17.00 ⎫   |           |         |        |
| 18.00 ⎬ — * |         | 7.00    |        |
| 19.00 ⎭   |           |         |        |
|           |           |         |        |
| 15.00 ⎫   |           |         |        |
| 16.00 ⎬ — * |         |         | 7.00   |
| 17.00 ⎭   |           |         |        |

| Dep.  |         |      |
| Nice  |         |      |
| 20.00 | 7.00    |      |
| ,,    |         | 7.00 |

* Hour of departure dependent on vessel.

Seasonal services from Nice and Marseille to Ile Rousse and Calvi, from Marseille to Propriano, and from Toulon to sundry ports, are also listed in addition to the above. Now here are the return sailings:

| Dep.    |       | Arr.      | Arr. |
| Ajaccio |       | Marseille | Nice |
| 17.00 ⎫ |       |           |      |
| 18.00 ⎬ — * |   | 7.00      |      |
| 19.00 ⎭ |       |           |      |
|         |       |           |      |
| 20.00   |       |           | 7.00 |

29

| Dep. | | | Arr. | Arr. |
|------|---|---|------|------|
| *Bastia* | | | *Marseille* | *Nice* |
| 15.00 | | | | |
| 16.00 | — | * | 7.00 | |
| 17.00 | | | | |
| | | | | |
| 20.00 | | | | 7.00 |

* Hour of departure dependent on vessel.

It will be noted that most of these sailings are arranged to be overnight. For this reason, and because in the season they are crowded, I advise a first-class ticket with a *couchette*. A first-class single on one of these ships from Marseille to Ajaccio costs 40,68 N.F., to which is added another 12,97 N.F. *supplémentaire* as "taxes," whatever they are. Port-duty, tolls, and what-not, one supposes (mostly what-not). In addition to this a *couchette* costs 18 N.F. and is well worth it. Meals run to 10 N.F. or so. Marseille to Bastia is a slightly higher fare, Nice to Bastia (or vice versa) rather lower — the latter at present at 27,60 N.F. without tax. I should stress that these are prices at going to press and thus subject to augmentation, if anything. But  you should be able to get from London to Ajaccio by train and boat for not much more than £25.

Finally, your car. When did you last weigh your Austin in kilos? Well, have some idea of this before you set out because that's what the tariff is based on: up to 799 kilos your car transporation costs 91 N.F., from 800 to 1,199 it will cost 122 N.F., and so on up the scale accordingly. All these expenses (or *frais*), including a cosy berth for your car, can be paid for in the country of origin. There is a free baggage allowance of 30 kilos for each adult and 20 kilos for each child, excess baggage being charged at 2,65 N.F. for every 10 kilos or part.

Lastly, here are the C.G.T. offices in Corsica:

*Ajaccio:* Quai Lherminier (Tel.: 1-13, 0-82, 2-37).

*Bastia:* Chambre de Commerce, Rue du Nouveau-Port (tel.: 0-57, 2-62).

*Calvi:* Quai Kitchner (tel.: 8).

*Ile Rousse:* Avenue Joseph-Calizi (tel.: 35, 57).

*Propriano:* Quai de la République (tel.: 6).

(ii) From Italy:

There is at the moment one boat a week from Livorno to Bastia. It leaves on Mondays at midnight, arriving at Bastia at 7.00 a.m. the next morning. Usually a little bit before this. The Italian Tirrenia service handles the sailing, which is a much more convenient one than it sounds. I have taken it and been grateful for the late hour, since it enables one to get to Livorno from other points in Italy without the bother of having to spend the night there.

Actually one can get on board any time from ten on, after a good dinner at one of the excellent Livornese restaurants like Novelli in the Piazza Cavour or Acquaviva-La Serra sul Mare, which is just outside the town. One can then go to sleep before the ship sails, to be woken by one's steward on arrival the next morning. A first-class cabin is recommended on this run and is, indeed, absurdly cheap, less than the French charges quoted above. Cars may be taken, too. If and when this trip is made in daytime, I am told that it gives superb views of Monte-Cristo, Elba and Capraia. Should you, on the other hand, wish to travel from Corsica to the Italian mainland you will find the Tirrenia Agency in Bastia at no. 1 *bis* Rue du Nouveau-Port.

31

(c) *By Air:*

(i) From England:

This couldn't be simpler. In 1959 B.E.A. ran two flights a week to Ajaccio (none to Bastia). These left London on Tuesdays and Sundays at 8.25 a.m. and arrived in the Corsican capital at 11.30 a.m. The plane went on to Malta. There are further constant services to Nice, of course, from which you can hook up with Air France planes.

On Wednesdays and Fridays, there were B.E.A. flights back out of Ajaccio at 1.25 p.m., arriving in London at 4.45 p.m. The flights originated in Malta and seemed rather more crowded than you would perhaps expect. Round trip fare, Tourist Class, from London to Ajaccio was £48 18s. 0d. A 23-day excursion ticket is available on the flight leaving London on Tuesdays for £42 5s. 0d.

(ii) From France:

Flights abound. Here is the 1960 schedule of Air France services to Corsica:

| Day | Marseille (Marignane) | Ajaccio (Campo del Oro) | Bastia (Poretta) | Calvi (Ste. Cathérine) |
|---|---|---|---|---|
| Daily exc. Tues/Sun | 7.20 | 8.45 | | |
| Daily exc. Wed/Sun | 13.05 | 14.30 (snack) | | |
| Wednesdays | 15.00 | 16.25 | | |
| Sundays | 12.00 | 13.25 | | |
| Tues/Thurs/ Fridays | 7.40 | | 9.15 | |
| Mon/Wed/ Fri/Sundays | 13.25 | | 15.00 (snack) | |
| Mondays | 17.00 | | 18.35 | |
| Saturdays | 11.30 | | 13.05 (snack) | |
| Tues/Thurs./ Saturdays | 10.45 | | | 12.10 |

32

| Day | Nice (Côte d'Azur) | Ajaccio (Campo del Oro) | Bastia (Poretta) | Calvi (Ste. Cathérine) |
|---|---|---|---|---|
| Mon/Wed/Fri/Sun | 16.50 | 17.50 | | |
| Tues/Thurs/Saturdays | 7.30 | 8.30 (breakfast—cont. to Algiers) | | |
| Fridays | 11.20 | 12.20 (snack) | | |
| Mon/Wed | 7.30 | | 8.30 (breakfast—cont. to Algiers) | |
| Tues/Thurs/Sat | 16.50 | | 17.50 | |
| Fridays | 7.30 | | 8.30 | |
| „ | 16.00 | | 17.00 | |
| Tues/Thurs/Sat | 14.55 | | | 15.40 |

The on-to-Algiers flights are specified since they tend to be rather more crowded than the others. Round trip fare, Economy Class, from Marseille to any point on Corsica, is £11 2s. 0d. (153 N.F.); from Nice to anywhere on Corsica it is £7 7s. 0d. (102,60 N.F.). When booking, don't forget that some of the Air France (actually the Breguet 763) is equipped with two-tier seating; in which case, request a seat in the Upper Berth (or *Pont Supérieur*).

There are now twice-weekly services from Paris to both Ajaccio and Bastia; both flights take under four hours. At present there are no air services to Corsica from Italy. However, since airlines change their schedules annually, the above information is offered in the nature of a preliminary guide as to what you are likely to find on consulting your agent; the latest rumours as I go to press are that these services will be, if anything, stepped up.

33

In Corsica B.E.A. is agencied by Air France, with whom you should naturally confirm your return reservation at least forty-eight hours in advance. Get your hotel to do this for you if your French is not up to competing with the Corsican telephone system or you are bothered by the counter *(jeton)* it is necessary to buy to make a telephone work there. The Air France officials on the island are mostly young and courteous and many of them speak English well.

At Ajaccio the Campo del Oro airfield is close to the town and, if taking a bus, you will find that this leaves the central Place Foch some half-hour or so prior to departure time. As a matter of fact, a huge new road has recently been driven out to the field and it is also incidentally worth knowing that the airport has a surprisingly excellent little restaurant, should you (like me) prefer a decent meal on terra firma before taking off, rather than the cellophane-wrapped business that is offered aloft on the B.E.A. return run. In Bastia, where Air France holds out in the rather gloomy *gare,* note that the Poretta airport is further away, a matter of some seventeen kilometres from the town, in fact. Correspondingly earlier departure times by the Air France bus, therefore. At Calvi the field is once more close to the town. Now here are the three Air France offices in Corsica and I should say that the first-mentioned, in Ajaccio, is right opposite one of the most delightful markets imaginable — don't miss a stroll there!

*Ajaccio:* 3, Boulevard du Roi-Jérôme (tel.: 2-63, 10-76, 0-61).

*Bastia:* 6, Avenue Carnot (right in front of the station, that is; tel.: 11-32, 7-10, 8-21).

*Calvi:* Agence J. B. Pietri, Quai Kitchner (tel.: 8).

## 2. On The Island

(a) *By Land:*

  (i) By Car: (2)

"Get any thought of drive-yourself out of your mind, right in the beginning," reads some advice given in a recent issue of an American magazine to prospective motorists in Corsica, the reason advanced being the winding nature of the roads. I quote this at once simply because I disagree with the statement entirely.

Self-drive cars are, to my mind, the best way of seeing the country unless you can bring your own vehicle. Several of my friends would agree whole-heartedly with this opinion and indeed, simply because this kind of service has become so necessary there, Corsica now has the business well laid on. You need not worry about being over-charged. All you need worry about is reserving your self-drive sufficiently in advance; for this a deposit is required.

Of course, you will not find the roads up to the standard of British motorways or American "throughways" (I can't avoid the suspicion that U.S. motorists are hopelessly spoilt drivers when I see a recent issue of a magazine as sophisticated as *Esquire* seriously devoting an entire page to showing how to double-de-clutch)! Another American guide to Europe before me advises in general that "Renting a car for any period of time longer than a few hours is another way to go broke quickly." Again, I couldn't agree less. Forget these jeremiads.

---

(2)—See also the Section entitled "Motoring" on page 73.

On the other hand, I must agree that a chauffeur-driven car in Corsica would prove prohibitively costly for any length of time. But I cannot recommend too strongly the hire of a small drive-yourself vehicle of well-known make when you are there, if only for a few days. I repeat — *small*. The roads are narrow and a large car would be a nuisance in the mountains. No, this is far and away the best method of exploring Corsica and, above all, of making your own "finds." You can also safely hire self-drive scooters, while not everyone knows that nowadays most airlines will take bicycles as part of your baggage. Sample itineraries are listed in an appendix.

I myself have hired a self-drive car in Ajaccio and know that the system is thoroughly well established both here and at Bastia. However, there is as yet no "Pick-it-up-Here" and "Leave-it-There" service, as operates so excellently in America (where it is especially useful with luggage trailers). As remarked, no one is out to rook you, or put sawdust in your oil sump and say you ran a big-end, or some such trick. The best garages want their customers to come back, year after year, and they are out to encourage you to recommend other clients to them, too.

I say the best garages, note, because you should undoubtedly be careful in your choice of self-drive vehicles. If in doubt, ask "Essitac" in the Town Hall, or Hôtel de Ville, in Ajaccio for a list of recommended agencies. Yet this is not really necessary since both the Hertz and Mattei *location sans chauffeur* systems have outlets in Corsica and these names are recommendations in themselves in this field. Hertz is the huge American agency, of course, with a vast capital behind it. Mattei, a well-known name on Corsica, runs an equally lucrative chain of self-drive businesses throughout France (3). Both companies are obviously concerned to maintain their good names. You will be required to thump down a whacking deposit (or *cautionnement*) on taking over the car, but you can recover this when you have finished, or set it against your payment. Two other points of detail here: do make certain that the garage has full insurance (*assurance*) for the car, and try to haggle for a free limit (or *franchise*) of 100 kilometres a day. Some garages put this at 60 and it can make quite a difference if you do any distances.

As to choice of car and prices, I append a current tariff to these at the back of this book. As stated, the car should (and probably will) be small. Check your equipment with the mechanic (*mécanicien*) at the garage and get him to explain the operation of the car to you in detail, including such details one doesn't always think of at the time such as how the directional signals work. To do this you will need to know the French for a few parts, and to this end I append a brief glossary of these also. Plan to motor one day in or around the town where your garage is located before you start off round the coast or inland, just in case you should have any initial trouble. I have said that no one is out to swindle you but just in case your distance gauge or milometer is over-registering slightly, say, it would obviously avoid unpleasantness to drive back in and

(3) Mattei agencies can be found as follows in France:
*Paris:* 207 Rue de Bercy (Gare de Lyon; tel.: DOR. 75-91).
*Marseille:* 121 Avenue du Prado (tel.: 77-68-00).
*Lyon:* 100 Rue Pasteur (tel.: 72-03-80).
*Nice:* 5 Rue Halévy (tel.: 734-10, 827-72).

Hertz Europcar agencies, meanwhile, are almost too well-known to require listing, since they have been established in at least a hundred towns all over France by now. But here are some addresses for Hertz:
*Paris:* 43 Rue Bayen (tel.: ETO. 65-75).
*Marseille:* 25, 39 Cours Lieutaud (tel.: 59.53.32 and 20.98.30).
*Lyon:* 18 Cours Ar.-Briand (tel.: 51.57.59).
*Nice:* 8 bis Rue Maccarani (tel.: 847.63).

get the mechanic to check it with you against a couple of road signs or so. Don't forget to ask him to mark down on the oil intake when the car needs its next grease-job. Corsican roads bang all hell out of the springing and a small French car needs greasing (*graissage*) fairly often there — perhaps after some 1,200 kilometres or so.

Now here are the names of reputable self-drive garages on the island — I personally used M. Bianchi's in Ajaccio and was more than satisfied.

*Ajaccio:* Hertz Europcars, c/o Jean Bianchi, 16 Cours Grandval (tel.: 5-49).

(or consult Mme. Costa at "Essitac").

*Bastia:* Société Mattei, c/o M. Luiggi, 5-7 Rue du Nouveau Port (tel.: 7-99).

Hertz Europcars, Aéroport (tel.: 10-62).

Finally, the following British firm now has its own continental self-drive car network: Messrs. Maxwell Williams, 26 North End Road, London, N.W.11 (tel.: SPEedwell 1141).

(ii) By Train:

It is a strange and rather wonderful feeling suddenly to realize, after one has spent some time on Corsica, that one has never seen a train. It is as if that aspect of the industrial civilization had entirely passed the island by. I predict in fact that the already rather defeated-looking rail system there will gradually vanish and those iron monsters that have so scarred the rest of Europe become a thing of the past. Of course, this is already happening even in America, as a glimpse at the recent fortunes of leading rail shares there will soon show you. But in England we still strongly rely on our railways for transportation, they are a definite feature of our lives. Not so on Corsica and I, for one, enjoy a world which seems so little organized around this symbol of the nineteenth century.

All the same, fast Diesel and steam trains run between Ajaccio and Bastia and between both these towns and Calvi. The line between Ajaccio and Bastia through Corte can be seen from the road and is full of lovely views. This journey takes under five hours and a buffet-car is provided. During the season there are daily reciprocal services as follows:

| dep. Bastia | 5.15 (exc. Sundays) | arr. Ajaccio | 9.30 |
|---|---|---|---|
| ,, | 7.55 | ,, | 12.25 |
| ,, | 13.10 ( ,,    ,,   ) | ,, | 18.10 |
| ,, | 15.50 | ,, | 20.06 |
| dep. Ajaccio | 5.25 ( ,,    ,,   ) | arr. Bastia | 9.50 |
| ,, | 7.55 | ,, | 12.55 |
| ,, | 13.45 ( ,,    ,,   ) | ,, | 18.08 |
| ,, | 16.00 | ,, | 20.21 |

The journey from Bastia to Calvi takes some three and a half hours, while that from Ajaccio to Calvi (not recommended since it entails a change) takes five and a half hours. In the season trains leave Bastia for Calvi daily at 8.20 and 16.10 (except Sundays); on Sundays there is an 18.10 train. There's only one class on these trains which are quite small and sometimes, in August, fairly full of tourist and student groups.

(iii) By Bus:

The word is actually *autocar* or simply *car,* but do not be deceived, these are strictly the regulation charabanc, though modern and speedy. I mention this since I was misled owing to the fact that in Mexico there is a real car system for tourists, i.e. a fleet of large saloons carrying six passengers or so. But when an hotelier in Corsica refers to *un car* he means a bus not a car, which is *une voiture*.

This coach system is by now admirably arranged for your convenience in the island. There are a number of tours with attractive all-in rates, of which I have listed a typical one in the back of this book; British travel agencies are in any case well up in these and can give you all the information before you start. Some run convenient "all-in" tours, including bus excursions. In Corsica itself you will see dozens of "package" bus tours advertised both in Bastia and Ajaccio, and if in doubt I suggest you start by trying Corse-Tourisme, 5 Place Foch, in the latter town (tel.: 9-60).

If you are impecunious and adventurous, this then is the way to see Corsica. You can bus from one town to another —even the remotest mountain villages have some service of a sort—and stop off wherever and whenever you want to; this is how the locals travel, too, so that you will come into contact with some fascinating types. Don't be afraid of taking a reasonable amount of luggage on these buses; they are provided for it, some of the peasants you see seem to travel with all but the proverbial kitchen stove.

(b) *By Sea:* (4)

*Promenade en Mer,* as it's called. Beyond the purely local launches which will take you out to interesting grottoes and beaches, the C.G.T. passengers steamers ply around the West Coast. I recommend the lovely four-hour trip from Calvi or nearby Ile Rousse to Ajaccio, or vice-versa. However, these large boats sail fairly far off the coast and there is, in the season, a smaller launch (or *vedette*) which doubles between Calvi and Porto and takes you close in. There is also the C.G.T. service between Ajaccio and Propriano, which takes about two hours. And don't forget that you can cross from Bonifacio to Sardinia

---

(4) Strictly speaking, transportation *on* the island *by sea* would be what the *New Yorker* magazine calls the neatest trick of the week; but I thought it most helpful to arrange my information in this manner.

(with car, if you wish) in one hour! Tirrenia runs this service daily except Sundays in the summer. I have listed their office in Bastia above.

## PASSPORT — IDENTIFICATION

There are well-known Passport Offices in London (Clive House, Petty France, S.W.1), Liverpool (India Buildings, Water Street), and Glasgow (14 Blythswood Square); it is scarcely necessary to add that your passport must be valid. No visa is needed for travel to Corsica, which is a department of France. As I have never met, or even heard of, anybody losing his or her passport, I will skip the usual warnings of this order. H.M. Consul may be found in Ajaccio at the address, and telephone, listed in my section on that city below. It is obviously as well not to leave one's passport, tickets, and other papers in one's luggage. This is not because I believe there to be any petty stealing in Corsica. There is not. I have never heard of anyone losing a thing by theft there, it is quite out of character with the proud tone of the island, and most hotel servants are clearly models of integrity in this respect, except perhaps when they are imported from outside.

Carrying one's passport on one's person is a nuisance with the stiff, rather bulky British type, but it is just as well, and, if motoring, essential, to have some reputable form of identification on one. Corsican police take gloomy views of suspicious-looking characters who cannot identify themselves, but tourists will not be carted off to the local lock-up merely for being without means of identification.

One or two hints here might help, however. Learn the number of your passport and also the date and place it was issued (*délivré*). For British subjects this latter information is clearly stamped on one's passport (sometimes under the photograph) by the Foreign Office or, if one lives overseas, by the local British Consulate-General. It is often not so clear on the passports of other nationals; the place of issue is only lightly perforated on American passports, for instance, and I have frequently seen bedevilled "solid citizens" of that country frantically searching for this information in the lobbies of various hotels. Actually, a number is all that is shown on the cover of a U.S. passport.

The reason I bring this up is that passport details — including date and place of issue, as well as of one's birth — are required in Corsica on the so-called *Fiche de Voyageur,* or traveller's docket, issued to hotels by the police. If you travel around a good bit, moving from hotel to hotel, these *fiches* become nothing short of a damn nuisance, I find. I always forget the number of my passport. I always forget its date of issue. (I vainly *try* to forget the date of my birth). The result is that I have to wrestle unduly with these cards at each and every hotel I go to. My experience has been that some hotels insist on your filling out the police *fiches,* and some don't care at all. Some strike a tactful middle course by putting them out in a box in a sort of take-it-or-leave-it manner. In which cases I always leave it.


## CURRENCY — TRAVELLER'S CHEQUES

At going to press the obtaining annual foreign currency allowance is £250 per person on top of which you can take £50 sterling out with you also. The Treasury runs its foreign currency year from November 1st. Principal units of currency conversion into French francs are provided at the back of this book. Official rates of exchange can be weekly checked in *The Financial Times.* The difference between official and unofficial rates in pounds, francs, marks, and lire vary. On the whole, they are annually becoming more and more imperceptible. At present writing £1 sterling fetches 13,82 N.F. (5) in foreign exchange offices and banks; in this country you can sometimes get a higher rate per £1. You are allowed to take an unlimited amount of French francs into France or Corsica with you; you are allowed to leave with only two hundred.

The method of protecting one's money by carrying one's needs in the form of traveller's cheques is now fairly universally adopted. I labour this rather obvious point since it was not so after the last war in Europe, when hoteliers and their like trusted them less and visibly brightened at the sight of banknotes of the land, preferably "greenbacks" or dollar bills. Nowadays traveller's cheques are everywhere accepted and one is clearly advised to carry any substantial amount of money in them, noting down the serial numbers on a separate sheet.

I say any substantial amount because, with French regulations concerning importing currency as they now are, I seriously wonder if it isn't more advisable to take one's needs out in francs. At least up to £50 worth, surely. Remember that banks charge for dealing with applications for these cheques, as well as for the cheques themselves (usually 8d. each £2 cheque). I should also add the following warning here.

There are at the moment virtually only two places in which traveller's cheques can be cashed in Corsica *at the official rate of exchange*. These are the banks in Bastia and Ajaccio; in the former town there are two banks, the Banque de France and the Société Générale. In Ajaccio

---

(5) The " New " or " Heavy " Franc came into general use on 1st January, 1960, on the basis of one New Franc to one hundred Old Francs.

43

there are branches of these two banks, both in the heart of the town just off the main Cours Napoléon, and also the Banque de Commerce. The banks close at noon.

Apart from them your traveller's cheques will be cashed for you by hotels *at a discount*. Small, but still . . . Moreover, the hotels that will do this are relatively few and far between. It is as well to know this because the general form is for the encashing hotel authorities to smile affably and say reassuringly, Oh yes, they'll certainly change traveller's cheques for you.

At the official rate (*cours*)? you ask suspiciously. *Mais bien sûr*, they indignantly reply. Of course.

Yet what comes out of the eventual, brow-wrinkling additions is not the official rate at all. It is the official rates less a small percentage for what the hotel managements shruggingly refer to, when pressed, as bank charges. Now admittedly this clip is a small one; nevertheless, for some of us every penny is precious and you may well reasonably object to losing a few drinks needlessly in this manner. When you are cashing largish amounts, as I sometimes had to, the percentage concerned can become a real source of irritation. And one of my golden rules on holiday is not to let myself get rattled by petty details of this sort.

If you are travelling around Corsica, therefore, either cash well in advance at Bastia or Ajaccio, or bring over plenty of francs with you from London. Practically speaking, the day of the currency "fiddle" which was such a feature of post-war Europe is now over in the Western democracies at least, and you will not find yourself gaining much ground these days by buying francs in

Switzerland or wherever (6). Even the almighty dollar is not nearly as in demand as once it was, and no longer guarantees for its bearer those looks of obsequious awe it elicited around 1946 and 1947. There is, then, probably a small gain to be made over very large sums by buying outside French territory, but most readers of this book will be precluded by Treasury restrictions from taking such out with them anyway.

In this connection, let me reiterate: France at present allows an unlimited amount of currency to be taken into the country. It only permits 200 N.F. to be taken out and, unlike the comparable control in Italy, this restriction is nearly always enforced. I have never once left France in the past eight years (and I have been there almost annually) without being questioned by a Customs official —sometimes a woman, but generally a man—as to the amount of French currency I was carrying.

The question is often a courteously casual one, as if the whole matter were entirely academic, and at the little Ajaccio airport it is most apologetically put to you, but don't be deceived — it is in earnest. Thus, budget accordingly. It may be a nuisance, especially if one has left a largish bill to the last day, but 200 N.F. is still some £14 odd and represents nothing like the inconvenience we impose on foreign travellers by limiting them to £10 out of our country, more particularly when it is remembered that nowadays transatlantic excess baggage at nearly £1 a kilo may well run to a last-minute amount of this or more.

At all events, a fairly general principle in Corsica should be to keep plenty of cash on hand. This applies especially

(6) About the only wangle worth while that still obtains is to buy transportation *in France* with francs you have bought in London banks. This can still save you money, but it has other obvious inconveniences attached to it.

to motorists, of course. Finally, always check up with your travel agent as to the amounts of local currency allowed in and out of each country you are visiting; nowadays banks often supply this information in a useful booklet in which exchange tables are set out in convenient detail. Currencies are subject to last-minute variations, of course.

## INSURANCE

It is nowadays both easy and inexpensive to take out baggage and sickness-casualty insurances. I always do it. Over a short period it amounts to very little extra on one's whole holiday outlay, more specially if you can simply extend a current policy for these needs. And it is well worth it for the sense of relaxation and relief from worry it can provide. Travel agents will handle this for you, as a rule.

Our transatlantic cousins insure themselves against almost everything, even against bad weather "on vacation," but the price of these policies is, in a word, absolutely out of this world. Be quite certain, however, as suggested above, about your car *assurance* on the island.

## HISTORY

The history of Corsica has been an extremely painful one. Moreover, it will always remain a particularly difficult one for the outsider to assess or "pot" satisfactorily since, the country having been deprived until quite recently of any real sense of cultural identity, one perforce approaches it through the writings of foreigners. The majority of these records are French, of course, and admirably unbiassed as many of them are, they do treat the island from a certain angle.

Yet the Corsican schoolboy who today translates Seneca's wilfully ghastly description of the island (one written designedly to mitigate his exile) (7) knows in his bones that there is another, unwritten history, one of long and indeed agonized resistance to outsiders. Let us English hope that he discovers a more sympathetic spirit during his English lessons, when his teacher could show him Boswell's writings on the island.

This feeling of an unwritten, subterranean history which is the true repository of indigenous values can be found in a number of minority cultures. Mexico would be one, although the contributions of the two countries to world history could scarcely be compared. At any rate the lack of a cultural outlet itself often fosters in the social organism an understandable suspicion, even a scorn, of the outsider, or "gringo."

It still seems to me the merest courtesy to know the rough outlines of the development of a country one intends to visit and, because the susceptibilities of Corsicans are easily offended by ignorance of this nature, I propose to spend a few pages on the country's background (see also my chronology of main events at the back); it would surely be rather poor manners to ignore the name of the owner of a park into which one had been invited to ramble. However that may be, the three great names in Corsican history which all visitors to the country ought to know are, in chonological order: Sampiero Corso, Paoli, and Napoleon Bonaparte. There is a small bust of, and memorial stone

(7) According to tradition Seneca was exiled to Luri in Cap Corse for seven years (43-49); he did not like Corsica and the story goes that local peasants whipped him once with nettles for indulging in excessive intimacy with one of their girls. Seneca's Tower at Luri may still be seen. It is a hard climb up but worth a try for the superb views its elevation affords on either side of Cap Corse.

to, Paoli (8) in Westminster Abbey, while Napoleon (according to one of these bedazzling computations one takes on trust) is said to be the most written-about figure in world history after Jesus Christ. Do not admit to an Ajaccien that you have failed to see his birth-place.

First of all, it is of paramount importance to understand that Corsica has had almost continually to live under the shadow of some self-appointedly superior civilization. This has bred a tradition of resentment and solidarity in the national psyche, reinforced by a natural isolation (re-emphasized in the last war) not so evident in a minority culture such as that of Mexico, which developed in a more proximate relationship with its mainland, despite the geographical distance involved. Alongside this tradition grew up, of course, a strong habit of violence. As far as the resumé which follows here goes, and it cannot go deep, it should be emphasized that the sundry overlords under whom Corsica suffered simply viewed the island as a prestige colony, an acquisition in the sphere of influence rather than of wealth. Consequently even less care was taken of Corsica than, say Mexico or, closer to it, Sicily, from which countries the dominant exploiters found they were able to draw certain natural resources of value.

The external rule of Corsica, that is to say, was inaugurated on a "couldn't-care-less" basis, and it was this insulting attitude, more than any other, which threw up a reciprocally lively tradition of violence, world-famous now since it has been romanticized in stories of vendetta and bandit. The family vendetta is said not to be quite dead,

---

(8) " One of the most eminent and most illustrious characters of the age in which he lived."

but the bandit certainly is. (9). So also, as far as peripatetic visitors may go, is any unusual violence. That is definite. Ever since it gave the world Napoleon, Corsica has lost much of the chip on its shoulder; its psychology towards France is now perhaps even a mildly patronizing one at times. We were kept under for centuries, the Corsican must subconsciously remind himself, but when we produced a man for you, what a man! In fact, *we* produced modern France! Watching a televized soccer match between France and another country in a Bastia bar once — and soccer is nearly as popular there as *le catch* — I was pityingly informed by several local aficionados that if only France had played a certain Corsican goalkeeper . . . etc., etc. But it is in this spirit that Corsicans will seriously remind you that theirs was the first French territory to free itself from the Nazi yoke after the last war. And historically it is important to bear in mind that the country was treated with scant respect by the outside world from the start.

This start seems to have been vague even to early historians. Not until 1810, in fact, were megalithic remains noted (by Mathieu in *Mémoires de l'Académie Celtique*) and even the astute Prosper Merimée, as visiting Inspector of Historical Monuments there thirty years later, appears to have been uneasy about the island's origins. Since those dates a number of prehistoric dolmens or menhirs have been dug up, huge stones showing human arrangement or sculpting. As a result of these diggings (originally done in the teeth of a superstitious peasantry), it is now generally conceived that the early evolution of Corsica was one common to the whole Mediterranean basin.

---

(9) I have seen an altogether engaging form of " free-pass," issued as recently as 1935 and stamped, under the signature, with all the gravity of officialdom, " *Bandit* "!

Doubtless it was, but the most recent archaeological findings — those at Filitosa, which proceed as I write and to which I shall return below — may well add an unsuspected postscript of sophistication to primitive Corsican man. The latest Filitosa menhirs to be unearthed, to which several magazine articles have already been devoted, (10) are said to be the oldest in Europe, circa 3,000 B.C. They are more than worth a visit.

But, being small, Corsica has not proved rich in remains of the external civilizations which later colonized it. Both bronze and iron ages are scantily represented, there have been fairly few Etruscan discoveries (though skin-divers may soon contradict me here), and even the relatively advanced Roman settlement is attested only by a few coins, urns, and the foundations of the usual praetorian houses.

Legend has it that the island got its name from a Ligurian woman called Corsa, who followed her stray heifer into the sea all the way to the lovely island. Alternatively, you may believe that Hercules sent his son, Cyrnos, to Corsica and this is a name to be encountered often on the island today; the Greek word for Corsica — Kalliste — is equally common, *la Belle des Belles* as the French translate it, and it it used for several hotels and restaurants, as well as standing for a celebrated vineyard.

In the sixth century B.C. Greek installations were in fact made on the eastern seaboard, creating the so-called colony of Alalia. In turn, Etruscan sea domination resulted in the arrival of a new influence, later superseded by Syracusan and Carthaginian landings. *Portus Syracusanus*

(10) V. *Etudes Corses*, nos. 7-8, 1955. Subsequently to this an excellently illustrated article appeared, as ff.: Capitaine Roger Grosjean, in *Sciences et Avenir*, no. 118, décembre, 1956 (this *revue mensuelle*, should any readers be interested, is edited from 14 Rue Princesse, Paris VI).

was the name given by early geographers to both Porto-Vecchio and Bonifacio in the south.

From 260—163 B.C. Roman power began to substitute for the above. Taking to their mountains, the Corsicans seem to have resisted the initial Roman depredations very stoutly and it is said that the spirit of autochthonous independence which has always been such a feature of the island mentality found its real origins in this long struggle against Imperial might.

That there must have been considerable organization in their resistance by this time is attested by the fact that in a single engagement, in 173 B.C., the Corsicans are recorded as having lost 7,000 men. Soon after this they were united, under Pax Romana, in a single colony with Sardinia, with which country their relationship has since been fraternal. Pliny mentions thirty-three administrative areas in Corsica, and Aleria, which is now being excavated, was a town of between 15 and 20,000 inhabitants. The existence, indeed the strength, of Christianity early in the island is meanwhile witnessed by the martyred Saint Julie, whose breasts the Romans (some say the Vandals) ripped out and threw on to a rock. This rock, near the delightful village of Nonza in Cap Corse, immediately ejaculated two miraculous fountains, whose waters flow today.

Vandals and Goths who succeeded the Romans were duly ousted by elements of the Byzantine Empire, which continued to treat Corsica and Sardinia as an administrative unit. In the eighth century the island was grossly pillaged by Moors, Saracens, who only abandoned the country in 1014 before a coalition of Pisan and Genoese forces, leaving behind them, as it were, the famous black head first adopted for the coat-of-arms of the island in the eighteenth century by Théodore de Neuhoff, first (and only) "King" of Corsica. Paoli, too, when subsequently

51

creating a national mint, struck silver and copper coins bearing this now familiar Moorish profile with the white bandeau round the forehead. It is an icon of the island that can be seen everywhere there today.

This decisive intervention by the nascent Italian principalities of Pisa and Genoa charted the course of the country's fortunes for many centuries to come. From this moment Pisa and Genoa fought for the country, the former town being originally presented with it by the Papacy in 1077. This rivalry of two Italian feudalities at the expense of a perpetually oppressed island population virtually accounts for the Middle Ages in Corsica.

Under, at first, Pisan control the economy of the island was awoken and a clerical feeling permanently established. Throughout this struggle, too, the spirit of Corsican independence began to articulate itself through both local senior families and what were called *caporali,* often appointed from outside but sometimes citizens cast up locally to organize this spirit under a standard. And this sense of liberation seems to have been both national and social from the start, both against the dominant imperialist pretension, that is, and also against the sometimes restrictively feudal senior families.

In passing, it may today seem that a country with what was for so long an uninterruptedly revolutionary tradition, which knew its Zapata (if I may be allowed to pursue the Mexican analogy) in Sampiero and even an attempt at a thoroughly communist enclave in the fourteenth-century Giovannali sect, should today be celebrated for its political conservatism. I do not myself know the answer, which must in any case remain highly opinionative; it may be that this very conservatism Corsica presently expresses conceals a residue of true liberalism of which its critics are unaware. On the other hand, the Church influence may have proved over the centuries a politically hardening one, and thus be responsible for this dislike of change on the social level there; but I do not myself see why this need necessarily be so. Or perhaps Corsica's politics can best be looked at as simply a manifestation of that sense of stability conferred by living on an island, cut off from transient concerns, and in continual touch with the eternal verities. Conservatism is not necessarily extreme social reaction, as it is so often held to be. In any case, it is not the business of the outsider to interfere in local politics. I might add that I was in Ajaccio myself just after the Gaullist *coup*. The whole place was extraordinarily quiet, evidently the populace still sipped their aperitifs outside the cafés and bars while a handful of officials changed offices in the préfecture. But lurid newspaper reports put off many tourists that summer.

So at first, to return to my point, the Holy See favoured Pisa as Corsica's protector. There occurred the fairly usual pontifical scuffles until, in the twelfth century, Innocent II gave a good portion of Corsica over to Genoa in an act of attempted pacification. From this moment Genoese influence was strong. As far as the average tourist goes, it will be seen daily, momentarily, in the succession of Genoese round towers, nearly a hundred in all, placed on dominating positions along the coastline in order, originally, to give beacon warnings of approaching raiders and pirates.

These towers are often held up as highly picturesque, and are so indicated on maps; but I should say that in appearance they do not differ from the characteristic Medici towers to be found in Italy, notably on the islands there. Still, it is true that those in Corsica are generally seen on the most delightful promontories and were mainly built around the turn of the sixteenth century — the Tour des

Sanguinaires near Ajaccio, for instance, which almost every visitor sees, was constructed in 1550. You can wander freely into any of these old towers.

It is said that Genoa is despised in Corsican memory ("our women were good enough to deal with them"), but I can't say I personally found or felt any evidence of this. It may be so, however. In any event, the first Corsican patriot to try to impose any sort of collective pattern of national liberty under external oppression arose at this juncture of circumstances. He was a Bonifacien Lord, Sinucello de la Rocca, son of Gugliemo de Cinarca, killed in a vendetta by his nephews who were in turn wiped out by his more direct descendants. Under the name of Giudice (Judge) de Cinarca, Sinucello tried to play Pisa against Genoa in a desperately abortive attempt to liberate something of the country. After several skirmishes he was exiled for safe keeping to Genoa in 1299.

In the fourteenth century Genoese control was threatened by a new Mediterranean power, that of Aragon with whom, after the plague of 1347-48 had carried off a third of those living in the country, Genoa indulged in protracted diplomacy of a filibustering nature. In 1390 their Doge, feeling threatened by Milan, offered temporarily to lend his suzerainty to France with the result that Corsica became for the first time a quasi-French dependency. Vincentello of Istria, near Sollacaro in the south, intervened in this rivalry, conquered the island, and incidentally constructed the fine citadel at Corte. By 1421 even the contemporary Genoese memorialist Stella refers to Vincentello as the ruling power in the land. Captured by the Genoese, Vincentello was executed under what came to be known in France as the guillotine. The partisans he left behind him were treated mercilessly. But his is another name that still lives in Corsica today.

Genoa now entrusted the affairs of this indigent and troublesome island to the Bank of San-Giorgio. The Bank built a fortress at Ajaccio (into which at first only the most privileged Corsicans were admitted) and put the island's economy better on its feet, yet at the same time afflicted the peasantry with all the rigour characteristic of the death-throes of feudalism. To anticipate local uprisings, for example, the bearing of any form of arms was forbidden. As a result the Barbary corsairs ran riot, landing almost at leisure where they would. Algajola received a permit for four firearms, needed urgently against bears. It was razed shortly afterwards. Thus this epoch saw the first of Corsican emigration on any considerable scale. It remains a feature of the present day, the census having sunk by 75,759 between 1937 and 1956, while the 1946 passenger port statistics showed 6,411 more departures than arrivals. Depopulation of this kind results in over-population (by the non-productive old and very young) and when to this decline in man-power are added the balance of three times as much import material over its exports, a continual excess of births over deaths, and falling harvesting and fishing figures, the problem of poverty will be seen to be just as great as it ever was. For this reason, more than any other, Corsica has felt herself in recent years the "forgotten department" of France.

But at the above low point in the country's fortunes Sampiero Corso was born — at Dominicacci, near Bastelica, the mountain village in the heart of the island, where his humble home was resurrected from Genoese flames and may still be seen today under the inscription (in Corse), *To the most Corsican of all Corsicans.*

Sampiero da Bastelica seems to have been an authentic revolutionary, a breaker-down, unlike the milder Paoli, who was a social architect, a builder-up. After a military career in France Sampiero returned to troubled Corsica in 1547 and married Vanina d'Ornano, a patrician lady he later strangled (the while characteristically begging her pardon) for staining, as he supposed, both her patriotism and her marriage bed. With a formidable military reputation behind him, a friend of Bayard and reputedly "worth 6,000 men," Sampiero awoke his compatriots against their Genoese overlords and in fact freed his country for the first time under nominal French rule in 1553.

The Genoese, led at sea by Andrea Doria and with German levies, razed coastal town after town, outlawing Sampiero and hunting him into the hinterland, but on the 17th September 1557 the Consulte de Vescovato formally incorporated Corsica under the French crown. Two years later, at the treaty of Cateau-Cambrésis, France renounced Corsica (mainly as a result of internal factions) and broke Sampiero's heart and strength. Nearly seventy years old, he was tricked into an ambush (not dissimilar to the one in which Zapata met his end) in January 1567. "Thank God," the Governor wrote to the Genoese Senate then, "this morning I put the head of the rebel Sampiero on a stake at the entrance to Ajaccio, and one leg on the bastion. I was not able to get together the rest of the body because the horsemen and soldiers each wanted a piece, to stick on their pikes as trophies."

So perished Sampiero, and the Genoese were at last compelled to take an active part in organizing the country they had so rudely annexed. But it was now a harsh rule — a decree of 1612, for example, forbidding any Corsican to hold public office — for Genoa felt correspondingly insecure as she declined. Discouraged, Corsica now sank into a lethargy, a social sleep rendered the more impotent by the Genoese policy of denationalization — *"Les étrangers en Corse et les Corses hors de Corse!"* was their motto. It was not until 1729 that the Corsicans could re-summon their energies to rise once more against Genoa. They did so largely on the immediate score of unjust taxation and in 1735 declared themselves independent under a six-member junta elected by the populace. On the 12th March 1736 a ship put in to Aleria bearing an imposing, bewigged figure clad in a furred, scarlet cape, with a Spanish sword at his side and a cane in his hand.

This was the celebrated Théodore de Neuhoff, mentioned above, an impecunious Baron who took it into his head to become King of Corsica, and was so acclaimed on the 15th April 1736! For this preposterously unlikely figure deceived the Corsicans (who had never seen such opulence as he displayed) into believing that he was a man of substance — until the Genoese sat up and took notice, whereupon he fled the island in ecclesiastical disguise, showering out noble titles as he went. He later endured a number of vicissitudes and ended up in, amongst other places, a debtor's prison in London. In fact, when asked for collateral, Théodore cited "my kingdom of Corsica" and this the London tribunal solemnly registered for his creditors. The Baron was bailed out by Horace Walpole and died in poverty in London in 1756. Voltaire had much fun at his expense, putting the following words into his mouth at the dinner for six deposed monarchs in *Candide:* (11)

I am Theodore; I was elected King of Corsica; I have

---

(11) A recent English biography of Théodore may be turned up as follows: Aylmer Vallance, *The Summer King. Variations by an Adventurer on an Eighteenth-century Air.* London: Thames and Hudson, 1956. A good book, but considering the colourful subject and skilful author, somewhat disappointing. Théodore's son, Frederick, wrote a book of memoirs of Corsica.

been called Your Majesty and now I am barely called Sir. I have coined money and do not own a farthing; I have had two Secretaries of State and now have scarcely a valet; I have occupied a throne and for a long time lay on straw in a London prison.

By this point, however, naval power had reached a point at which Corsica was seen to be of great strategic importance in the Mediterranean. The French, loath to let the weakening Genoese appeal (as seemed likely) to Austria, "lent" them a small army of subjugation and followed up this "mission of conciliation" with a few resident Marquises. After which they retired. England cleverly saw the importance of Saint-Florent, in the north, as a naval base from which Toulon could be watched and, in the uncertainty of the island's affairs, bombarded and captured Bastia in 1745. These forays into their country from outside once more stiffened the spirit of Corsican independence, which became incarnate this time in Pascal Paoli.

Under Paoli's leadership Corsica became genuinely mistress of herself and, by a popular vote of 13th July 1755, he was elected General of the country. This brief period under Paoli is considered by most Corsicans as their moment of greatest glory. Paoli founded a government based on democratic principles far ahead of his time, established educational units beyond what was to be the University of Corte, where local aspirations could find intellectual respectability, and created a kind of military truce with France, to whom Genoa had once again appealed for assistance. Paoli was directly inspired by Rousseau and some of his constitutional reforms do strike one today as hopelessly utopian (particularly those limiting periods of office), but he was undoubtedly a great man and imposed civil society on a country of now some 122,000 inhabitants.

But France needed Corsica for its crescent naval pretensions. Genoa ceded, sold, its rights to France, and the French Comte de Vaux crushed Paoli's poor forces at Ponte Nuovo in 1769, the year in which, two months later, Napoleon Bonaparte was born in a side street in Ajaccio. Paoli fled to England.

From this point on France sought to integrate Corsica into her own country, of which of course she is now a department. After the outbreak of the revolution Louis XVI recalled Paoli and gave him command of Corsica. An old man (and Corsicans age fast), Paoli was put in a quandary, once back in his beloved country. He was a committed republican but pinned his hopes for complete independence — against those of the Bonapartists on the island — on coming to terms with England. He surely hoped that it would thus eventually be easier to liberate Corsica from English, rather than from French, dominion. At Paoli's instance, Admiral Hood and the young Captain Nelson appeared in Corsican waters.

In command of a naval brigade Nelson blockaded Calvi (where he lost his eye), reduced Saint-Florent and Cap Corse, and dropped anchor in Bastia harbour on the 19th February 1794. Since he was an exact man, Nelson's correspondence concerning Corsica makes extraordinarily interesting reading today and, surprisingly enough, I have only met with the warmest regard for his name there. Saint-Florent seems as if flattered by his visit! In any case, under the pressure of this astute naval officer, Paoli ceded Corsica to England, for which country he himself embarked in 1795 and where he died in 1807, his ashes being returned to Corsica in 1890. Sir Gilbert Elliot, later Earl of Minto, was created Viceroy of the island. But in

59

1796 the British Government decided to evacuate Corsica. In October a reluctant Nelson, who had seen the value of its bases, embarked the last.

Napoleon lost no time in welcoming his island back into the French fold. The Directory sent Miot de Melito and Joseph Bonaparte to land at Erbalunga in December of the same year. It must not be imagined, from present-day sentiment, however, that all Corsica was devotedly Bonapartist. Far from it. With the Bourbon Restoration the Corsicans became, what they have whole-heartedly remained, loyal Frenchmen, if Corsicans above all.

When France fell in 1940, Mussolini turned his aspirations on the island to which he sent troops after the Allies had made their first North African landings in 1942. In fact, Mussolini's imperialist pretensions at this time were reflected in several "official" pamphlet publications of the Italian Library of Information, still on record, of course. One of these, called *Corsica,* lies before me as I write, and makes what one can only call pretty spooky reading today; it shows that the Italian dictator was definitely out to reconquer this "prisoner of the Mediterranean," suppressed as it was by "a sizable garrison of coloured troops" from France, while "Pasquale di Paoli" (*sic*) is represented as an Italian patriot ahead of his time! (12).

The Corsican resistance was stiffened during the war by clandestine landings — such as that from the famous submarine *Casabianca,* which escaped from Toulon — in spite of strict enemy surveillance. In 1943, with the fall of

---

(12) If you read Italian, try also in this same context Andrea Pasqualine's really fantastic *Il Martirio della Corsica, isola italiana* (Firenze: Vallecchi, 1939).

Mussolini, the Corsican partisans most bravely arose and, with minimum outside assistance, captured Bastia and liberated their country on the 4th of October, the Germans needlessly blowing up no less than one hundred and twenty bridges as they left (13).

## LANGUAGE

There are two languages spoken in Corsica: French and Corsican or, as it is called, Corse. French is the "official" language of the island and it is all you need to know. The pronunciation of Corsican place-names is generally speaking more often French than Italian, but this varies considerably. Thus I first went around calling Cargèse by its Italian phonemes — i.e., Kar-*gay*-zay. No one knew what I was talking about, until I pronounced the place in the gently French fashion, Kar*jaise*. The Rue César Campinchi in Bastia, on the other hand, follows Italian usage, as to the last two syllables, which are said *pinky;* the same is true of Porto-Vecchio, which is pronounced precisely as any Italian might expect to hear it in his country. Yet the village of Sainte-Marie-Siché, to give only one instance, breaks these rules, the last word being said *si-chay*. Again, Bonifacio is pronounced with the final *c* soft, as it would not be in Italian and as it is, contradictorily enough, with Ajaccio. Ajaccio is pronounced by *most* local Corsicans Ah-*yah*-cheo, and the Ajacciens are Ah-yah-*chines*. But this, too, varies, depending on how Corse you are; the French element often pronounce the capital with the French *c,* and really the best advice I can give is simply to use what might normally

---

(13) For an interesting article by an American who landed with the U.S. troops in August 1944 v.: Richard Joseph, "Path of Contrasts: The Mediterranean," *Esquire,* September, 1955.

be the French pronunciation, until you learn at first hand the local variants.

For French is the "official" language, spoken everywhere (often with an Italianate or *midi* accent), and understood in shops, hotels, and so forth. France proper is usually referred to, as a matter of fact, as *le continent*. Do not be unduly cast down, however, if some dazzling French idiom you have been rehearsing for days is met with a blank look. Corsicans are not, on the whole, very used to foreigners and are, I think, somewhat slow in adapting their ears to new habits of speech and delivery. They themselves completely lack the melodious Parisian chirrup in their French, which they deliver with set expressions diametrically opposed to the mobile phrasings of the Italian whose intonations, nonetheless, haunt their vowel sounds. But for this reason, since French is the language used throughout, and because all English tourists nowadays have (or should have!) a working knowledge of their neighbour tongue, I have not thought it necessary to encumber this volume with any linguistic aids, except in the cases of two special fields, those of motoring and cookery. With the opportunities there are for learning French today, with tools like Hugo and Cortina at hand, I felt it would be insulting to add a list of elementary phrases here. Still, I do try to drop French equivalents of unusual and necessary words into parentheses in the text as I go along.

Lastly, I should add that we English are unfortunately notorious for our lack of linguistic ability, and this impression I think it absolutely essential to dispel as soon as possible. It is, philologically speaking, a phenomenon that goes hand in hand with a nation's period of imperialist pretensions, and we haven't been alone in the attitude by any means. Basically, the expression is one of cultural superiority — why should we speak your language when you can learn ours? The era of Spanish grandeur, for example, was responsible for Spanish being spoken all over the civilized world. To see how influential a language is, in fact, a comparison between the present political influence of Spain and the semantical significance of its language (throughout all the Americas, after all) is highly revealing. And it is interesting to note that today, if there are worse linguistic offenders than we English, they are to be found in countries which subconsciously (or consciously) want their influence to expand, namely the U.S.A. and U.S.S.R. In short, try to speak some French. Put words together. Repeat phrases you hear from Frenchmen. I am *not* advising anyone to lift the bottle when I say that alcoholic release of the mnemonic processes is well-known (I have even read a learned article on the subject). But you may break the ice with your psyche if you make those first promised efforts to speak French after a damn good dinner!

What, then, is Corse? Corse is the indigenous language of the Corsican people, evolved over centuries and current before the French language was implanted from outside only at the end of the eighteenth century, for political purposes, and taught at the very colleges Paoli had founded to encourage native aspiration. You will not understand Corse. A very large number of the middle-classes in Corsica don't. It sounds like a mixture of French and Italian, with the emphasis on the latter, and roughly that is what it is. If you speak straight Italian well, by all means use it in Corsica. It will be understood by hotel employees, porters, taxi drivers, and in most shops and restaurants.

As a matter of fact, if you are sensitive to intonations, you will notice that in the interior French lies uneasy on the Corsican tongue; it is the "genteel" language, an imposition of the drawing-room, as it were, and a few Italian phrases will often appeal to the more down-to-earth of such people and draw a grin from them. Singers at night-spots, too, tend to alternate between songs in French and Italian: Dalida, for example, who sings her French (or did) in a very strong Italian accent, enjoyed enormous popularity in Corsica before she achieved real fame elsewhere.

I must finally insist that it would be erroneous to call Corse a dialect, if by that word you imply a corruption of a mother-tongue. When you are in Italy, for instance, you will talk Italian with the waitress who serves your table, and then hear her rattle off a generally unintelligible lingo to her pals at the back of the house. This is probably a dialect in the true sense.

But in Corsica there formed a linguistic amalgam which must be pretty well as old as French itself and which, in any case, exists on a fraternal basis with it. The Saracen influence characterized Corse long before any Frenchman ever saw the island. Note the Arab etymology of many of the place-names.

It is as well to emphasize this point since non-linguists tend to regard a dialect in the pejorative sense, that is, they look down on it. The comparison closest home might be the Doric, or Braid Scots. This language of the Lowlands (Lallans) formed in Scotland before the French invasion of England and cannot therefore be thought of as the comic oddity, the amusingly "couthy" corruption of King's English, it is so often represented as on the music-hall stage or, more indirectly, in novels according Scots characters lower-class or funny roles (Sir Walter the chief offender here, of course). No, Corsican has, just like the Doric, its own heroic genealogy. The fact that this has not

Ajaccio: from the Bois des Anglais.

Ajaccio harbour.

3.        The Château de la Punta (extreme right) near Ajaccio.

4.        Typical Calanches near Piana.

been eventuated into a literature must be laid in reproach at the feet of those who exploited the economy of the island for so long without educating its populace.

However, like Scotland, Corsica has certainly thrown up a profoundly original vernacular ballad. These are thick, vehement laments or love-songs, usually to a guitar, and they are like nothing else on earth. It is said to be very difficult now to find authentic Corsican minstrels (14). The area extending very roughly north-eastwards of Corte towards the coast, called La Castagniccia, is rumoured to be the last repository of the true Corse ballad. These ballads traditionally include the funeral chant for women mourners, called *Voceri,* and the famous chant of family vengeance, *Rimbecco.* What you and I will hear will chiefly be syrupy songs in bars, but even these adulterations can be moving enough.

As has happened with the Lallans ballad in Scotland, now that it has virtually died out cultural agencies have made a rush to put on tape the last surviving examples. The vanishing of linguistic eccentricities, such as Corse, only makes for increasing conformity in the world and it is dearly to be hoped that the French authorities will do all they can to preserve the Corsican vernacular.

## PEOPLE

Here is an abstract of what the Corsican people seemed like to outsiders in 1769:

In general, they are grave, serious and melancholy, in the midst of their vivacity, and they seldom laugh. The hardships of their country seem to occupy them exclusively and gives them a sombre, savage air. In their

---

(14) The French Government Tourist Agency usually tries to keep on hand a list of activities, such as folk singing, at the chief festivals celebrated by indigenous communities.

c

lean, intelligent faces you notice a certain stiffness. No amusements, no dancing, no *fêtes champêtres* . . . one might say of these Corsicans, whose skies after all are so light, clear and airy, what Renan said of the Bretons, that joy itself is a little sad with them. Fear of exploitation, tenacious and indomitable resistance characterize them. (15)

To this admirable general summary time has added few footnotes. The description remains exact enough, when you take into consideration social betterment and the decreased isolation of modern times. Since someone else has said it first, in short, an outsider like myself will perhaps seem less presumptuous in adding his own feelings rather along this line.

For the Corsicans are what the Scots call "dour." There is no doubt about that. This is most noticeable should you go there for the first time from Italy where the faces one meets are so extraordinarily expressive, of course, and where even the most humble of human beings seem gifted with a grace of manner that makes being swindled by them (and is one, really?) such a pleasure.

Tourists tend to meet employees — especially waiters, waitresses, porters, drivers, and the like. In these professions natural courtesy is at a premium. It wins hands-down in Italy, needless to say. And part of the enjoyment of any holiday worthy of the name is, to be sure, the feeling of being treated with that delightful deference, combined with inner dignity, one meets throughout places like Italy. I well recall an hotelier I know in that country finding himself pushed for help during one particular August rush; he solved the problem by sending out into a nearby street, where an olive-skinned lad of some thirteen years of age

(15) Colonna de Cesari-Rocca et Louis Villat, *Histoire de Corse*, Paris: Boivin, 1927, p. 226. My translation.

was punting a soccer ball about. In a matter of minutes this local goalie was converted into a white-coated waiter of enormous suavity and, even, at times, of a degree of supercilious *savoir-faire* it would take most of us years to affect.

Do not expect this in Corsica. Hotel staffs tend to be polite, but perfunctory. Faces do not smile easily, especially the men's — notice this trait in the strong countenances of the fishermen and also those shepherds who will be making down to the coasts from September on. I mention this point merely to prepare against disappointment. The first Corsicans I spoke to in my life gave me the impression of being extremely cross. But that this is a superficial impression I have learnt again and again, when returning on my tracks and meeting old acquaintances full of enthusiastic welcomes and great generosity. A French friend told me once, in this connection, that rather like the equally proud Spaniards, Corsicans are always afraid that the foreigner, particularly the Parisian, is looking down on them. I wonder.

One final aspect, here. "The character of the natives, notwithstanding the levelling and equalising effects of advancing civilisation, corresponds with the wild aspect of their country." Thus, Baedeker. But the old boy was writing years and years ago and, if one thing can be stated categorically today, it is that banditry is over in Corsica. Anyone who goes there expecting to find the kind of Corsicans that appear in nineteenth-century French romances is going to be right up a gum-tree, I fear.

## HOTELS

Each individual town or village covered below will be provided with some separate hotel listing, together with my own personal recommendations. New hotels are being constructed continually on the island; these brand-new edifices, with their stucco scarcely dry, look attractive enough, but the plumbing is sometimes less likely to be operating with the efficiency of older establishments. Most of my recommendations are in this latter field, tried-and-true places. Suffice it, then, to say here, in general terms, the following.

At the moment there is only one luxury hotel in Corsica: that is the Hôtel Napoléon-Bonaparte at Ile Rousse. Apart from this, most of the hotels are clean, comfortable, characterless, but quite satisfactory second-class hotels — far better, may I say, than one is often led to expect. Within this general category they vary, but not greatly.

The rooms are nearly always spotlessly clean, well looked after, and provided with running water, usually drinkable. Hot water is available at most, though not all, while at many it is available certain hours of the day only —when there's a rush to use it! Ask the management about these hours, if in any doubt. Corsican plumbing always seems to be going wrong and repairmen are dilatory (*"il est très difficile de monter une affaire ici,"* one hand-wringing hotelier put it to me in what might be called the understatement of the year). Towels are provided, but not soap, so bring your own.

For the standard of hotel obtaining a surprisingly large number of rooms are equipped with bathrooms. If you do not have your own bathroom, however, you can order a bath which is charged up on your bill (2,5 N.F. a crack, as a rule); it is also customary to slip a gratuity, or *pourboire,* into the ready palm of the good lady who prepares the holy of holies for you and who, in this case, provides soap. Rooms with communicating doors (*chambres communicantes*) also seem to be a fairly regular feature, if you wish. Laundry service is absolutely excellent at all these hotels. Provided the weather is fine, you can have anything you want done in a day or so by the chambermaid. But it's expensive.

Nearly all these hotels are *relatively* new establishments in the life of the island and there is simply not the large-scale hotel-business tradition you find in Italy or Switzerland. (Even Ajaccio, at present writing, has only 550 rooms available at the height of the season). They are designed to meet summer tourist needs and, as a consequence, few of them are equipped with good lounge facilities — least of all for writing letters, although you can nearly always request hotel writing-paper from the desk, or *caisse*. There are exceptions, but most hotels on the island are attuned to a living-out climate. Space is not wasted.

During the two months of rush, July and August, many of these hotels become very full indeed and I am afraid all too many of them have the feel of motels, catering to a rapidly itinerate clientele who will unprotestingly take anything they are given. All depends on the manager (or *patron*), of course. I have suffered silently in dining-rooms that resemble American diners with a flurried staff dashing past one's table at the double, periodically pausing to chuck down the next course that comes up on the menu, regardless of whether one had ordered it or not. As I say, this is not always the case, and it *never* is the case out of the season, but I might as well prepare you for the worst.

Next: Is it necessary to reserve in advance? During August, yes. However, most of the smaller hotels simply are not equipped to deal with protracted correspondence (that's why they like groups so much), and you or your travel agent may well find your letters unanswered. This is not indifference, so much as incompetence. I know of several leading hotels on the island failing to answer agency letters. If you do not get a reply, don't worry. It's nearly always possible (for a couple, at least) to find somewhere by telephoning from the first hotel you stay at and booking in advance there: for this reason you will find below that I provide telephone numbers as much as possible. Moreover, you will have got the "feel" of things after arrival and won't be tied down to commitments made in England. The hotel you stay at will always make these bookings for you and charge you for the telephone bill accordingly; it is as well to let them do it, in fact, since the Corsican telephone system is not simple. I might add that when reserving ask for a room with a view (*vue*); corny as this may sound in cold print, it's worth it every time.

One or two other points: Hotels with views, or near the sea, usually charge more than others. In this context the word *marine* is a useful feminine noun referring to the waterfront, jetty, sea-board, or what-have-you. Secondly, in the interior, you are almost certain to find somewhere to sleep, even in villages not listing hotels. Simply ask about, and you will find yourself directed to a house that rents rooms. Frugal, to be sure, but there is perhaps no better way of getting to know Corsican domestic life, of which the family is such a strong unit. If in any doubt, ask for the town-hall or mayor's house (*Mairie*) and there state your predicament. Staying at one of these inland villages, I should say, you might just be lucky enough to get to see a true Corsican marriage or funeral. And finally the local pension is much more likely to be open the year round. Some hotels close from October to April.

From the generally sublime to the practically ridiculous, let me counsel your taking, as well as the necessary soap mentioned, the following items for self-explanatory reasons: (a) one or two light steel coat-hangers, (b) Alka-

Seltzer — Corsican wine is high in alcoholic content, (c) some English toilet-paper, and (d) a combination tin and bottle-opener. Now for prices. How much are you likely to have to pay for hotels on the island? Are they cheap or costly?

The French Government Tourist Offices issue every now and then a listing of "Maximum Rates for Hotels in France." You will find something like this:

|         |    |                   | single | double |
|---------|----|-------------------|--------|--------|
| 4 stars | A. | Private Bath      | 29,50 N.F. | 44,00 |
|         |    | Running water only | 18,50 | 26,00 |
|         | B. | Private Bath      | 23,50 | 36,50 |
|         |    | Running water only | 15,50 | 22,50 |
| 3 stars | A. | Private Bath      | 18,00 | 27,50 |
|         |    | Running water only | 13,00 | 18,00 |
|         | B. | Private Bath      | 16,00 | 24,50 |
|         |    | Running water only | 12,50 | 17,50 |

Frankly, well-intentioned as these listings are, I fear that in Corsica at least they are not worth the paper they are printed on. Let me give a concrete example. The last time I was in Ajaccio I stayed at the excellent Solemare, a modest establishment rated 2 stars B and not even listed in the current Official Year-Book of the Tourist Hotels of Corsica. According to the French Government Tourist Guide I should have been paying, for my single room with running water only, a price of 7 N.F. Absurd! The bill in front of me shows that I actually shelled out 17 N.F. for the room daily. No extras. I was entirely happy to do so, but I advise you to scrap this guide, should it come your way or cross your travel agent's desk.

Instead, I suggest you get hold of the little folder (or *dépliant*) issued by "Essitac" in Corsica; this is annually re-edited and quite accurate. It lists every hotel of any consequence whatsoever and quotes minimum prices. Note that these are minimum, and for room only. They vary from about 12 N.F. (for any comfort at all) up to 46 N.F. at the Napoléon-Bonaparte.

Looking over my numerous bills I find that the best help I can give is this: if you stay at an hotel for a day or so only, you will be charged a rate for the room which should not average more than 30 N.F.; note that you pay a *room* rate in France, and its possessions, so that double room accommodation works out quite cheaply. Some double rooms cost no more than singles and the managements don't mind if you sleep six there (I wouldn't try this, however)!

On top of your room rate, allow 3 N.F. as a set price for breakfast (grotesquely expensive for what you get), 6 more for lunch, and 6 to 8 for dinner, exclusive of wines or extras, such as coffee. I stayed in several good hotels in Corsica in a double room with my wife for 20 N.F. a day, not counting food.

If you plan to stay for several days on end, take the *pension* rate, viz., with all meals included (or at least two), and you will effect a considerable saving, in my opinion. You can still find good complete pensions for 26 N.F., or perhaps a little more. You see, in most places in Corsica, food (and food prices) are fairly standardized. Further, I advise having hotel drinks put down on some chit or check, to be added to your bill at the end of the stay: this, to obviate the constant tipping of Tom, Dick, and Harry bringing you your *boisson*. Drinks can be ordered in any Corsican hotel, regardless of whether you see a bar or not — and one cut with the knife at the end of your stay, *ça suffit, hein, mon vieux?* One of my maxims (after painful experience in this respect in Italy) is always to try to avoid that situation where you tip about twenty people for approximately the same service. If you have a suit pressed, it's always seemed reasonable to me, the bloke who brings it back to your room is conceivably entitled to a *pourboire,* but not the bevy of bell-boys, each carrying the suit in separate sections (jacket, trousers, waistcoat) and in separate instalments, who so often arrive.

Finally, when paying bills or asking for numbers to be written down for you, don't forget that the French write a 1 like a 7. Their 7 is distinguished by the fact that it has its stalk crossed through. A 9 can looked damned like a 4 in French script, too. And get used as soon as you can to the *soixante-dix* (70) and *quatre-vingt-dix* (90) numeral system.

## MOTORING
(i) *In General:*

European automobilism has been enormously developed during the past two years. During the last August Bank Holiday alone, as I write, over 10,000 vehicles were embarked and disembarked at the car ferry terminal at Dover. Dozens of publications and printed books now cater to this growing public who take their holidays in cars; (15) others emerge as this guide goes to press. I shall try not to duplicate the information sources such as these provide, and instead to confine my advice mainly to automobilism in Corsica. At the same time, if you are contemplating doing extensive European motoring regularly, it might be a good idea to join one of the clubs that specialize in such motorists, as well as A.A. and R.A.C. I am a member of The Overseas Drivers Club (15, Bermans Way, London, N.W.10) and of The "G.B." Car Club (305a, Brompton Road, London, S.W.3.), both of which I warmly recommend for their many aids — litera-

(15) Two useful books in this field, still up to date, are Jerome Pastene's *Auto Guide to Europe* and Harry Lerner's *European Car and Travel Guide.*

ture, maps, advisory services, special insurance policies, so on — in the field of foreign touring. The Overseas Drivers Club features a combined R.A.C. membership; the "G.B." Car Club publishes an excellent quarterly called *Milestones*. Finally, I urge would-be motorists in Corsica to get a copy of the current French *Code de la Route*. (16)

Having said which, let me next counsel you to take with you, or hire on the island, a small car of fairly well-known make in good condition. Corsican roads are narrow, and likely to remain so in many cases, since they are cut out of cliffs. American cars of the larger variety remain virtually confined to the towns, like so many useless pterodactyls. Nor are the distances great, Corsica has about 1,000 kilometres of coastline and altogether about 2,000 kilometres of navigable roads in working order. Prospective motorists, then, are more than likely these days to know how to prepare both themselves and their vehicles for reasonably rough driving, so I shall not waste time by giving elementary advice in this direction. What I do offer are a few hints from considerable personal experience in motoring all over the island.

(ii) *Spares and Service Facilities:*

Unlike the petrol pump (*station service*), which is becoming more and more common in Corsica, garages for repairs (*réparations*) are still fairly few and far between. They are also nearly always full of work which is carried out on a competent but casual basis — don't bank on it being done by the date given. All depends on the temperament of the mechanic (*mécanicien*). I well remember watching one sail round Calvi bay for a couple of days with the wind just right. Very nice. The only thing

(16) Via a good book-seller or, if stuck, try: Georges Grail, 35 Rue de Grenelle, Paris 7.

was, according to his promises he should have been bent over my bonnet. And I very much doubt if the conditions most locals keep their cars in would satisfy the mildest police inspection anywhere else. If the brakes don't work, at least the horn will — such seems to be the general motto here, as in Algiers.

First off, then, make absolutely certain of those points —brakes and horn. You are going to need both badly in Corsica. To start with, the French use the horn for overtaking. Secondly, on the sinuous mountain roads the horn has to be in constant use as a warning, except at night when one uses one's headlights (*phares*), which should be in good dipping order. French cars often feature two notes on their klaxon — *de ville* for town use, and a stronger note, *de route,* for the open. (17)

Next, it is essential that your tyres should be in good condition. The puncture rate (*panne* or, simply, *roue*) is terrifically high on Corsican roads and I invariably travelled with *two* spare wheels. Once I needed both, too —right up in the mountains between Piana and Calvi. Check your jack (*cric*) and carry a pump. Most petrol places will gauge your tyre pressures for you. The standard recommendation for the Citroën Quinze (DS and ID 19 —family model), a car comparable with the medium-sized British saloon, is 1,450 kgs. per sq. cm. (or just under 21 lbs.) with four people aboard. I scarcely have to give experienced motorists advice in this regard — they know their own cars — but I personally prefer hard tyres for Corsican roads.

The French like a soft ride and in one village I found a thoughtful mechanic diligently lowering all my pressures;

(17) No hooting is allowed in Ajaccio, although, I fear, you will hear it. Always keep an eye out for the French crossed-through klaxon sign (*Zone de Silence*) when entering a town.

when asked why, he replied that I would shortly be climbing into hairpin mountain country and so he was giving me *pression pour les montagnes*. Nice and spongy for the mountains, in other words. This was precisely what I did *not* want because soft tyres puncture more easily, give you less m.p.g., and, although tyre pressures rise with heat, I like, and indeed recommend, a hard suspension on strange roads so that you know just what is going on. I have appended a tyre pressure conversion chart at the back of this book.

Headlights. The French drive by night on amber-hued lights. Take amber bulbs over with you or a fog transparency that will effectively mask the piercing (and much disliked) white of Anglo-Saxon headlights.

Have your springing well greased before setting out.

If you are not motoring in a well-known type of French car, carry spare sparking plugs (*bougies*). Your lubrication system should also be working perfectly since Corsican roads, at least the mountain ones, induce overheating (remove the thermostat, if you wish). Check your ignition and charging system and, a small point frequently forgotten in summer months, cast an eye over your windshield-wipers to see that they are working properly. When it rains in Corsica it usually pours in torrents and, if your *essuie-glaces* go on the blink, visibility will be a matter of a few yards ahead. Check your clutch and grind valves. (18)

Ajaccio and Bastia seethe with garages, but there are also good repair and greasing places at Calvi, Porto-

(18) For anyone taking a really fancy car to Corsica I commend the following spares kit: points, condenser, rotor, fan belt, petrol pump, diaphragm, generator brushes, starter brushes, flexible petrol line, fuses, radiator hose and clamps, road flare. You do *not* need, what some American autos now include, back-seat television, an ice-making unit, and perfume bottle.

Vecchio, Ile Rousse, Propriano, Bonifacio, and, in the interior, at Corte and Sartène. I have indicated prominent petrol pumps as I pass through towns below; these are on the increase, annually.

(iii) *Petrol:*

As United Kingdom regulations at present frown on the carrying out of the country of spare jerry-cans of British juice, and as you have to motor through France to get to Corsica on most itineraries, there is not too much you can do to cut down your costs on this item if you intend to kick off from England. However, Cook's and some banks do sell petrol cheques, of 10 N.F. each, and up to twenty-five are allowed to be taken out of the country. They save some money, but petrol (*essence*) is expensive in France. BP Plus costs a little over one New Franc the litre, or upwards of 7/6d. the gallon (non-tourist rate) — depending on how you have effected your currency exchange. The tourist rate works out at 4/10d. a gallon. A short table of liquid measures is provided in my appendix.

Petrol pumps are not nearly so few and far between in Corsica as they are often said to be. An experienced bus-driver once told me, as I set out inland for the Aïtone forest, that I shouldn't find one for miles and miles. Yet two in Evisa stared me in the face after only a few kilometres. All the same, caution is necessary since these pumps are not always full and for this reason I advise carrying a spare can, which you can top up with your favourite brand as you go along. A fairly high-octane fuel is, of course, advised for hot summer driving.

Somehow or other, the grape-vine of hotelier information always seems to know just which pumps have petrol and which don't. If you like, you can ask the desk to call up the pump you expect to pass and find out. These pumps are generally the property of cafés and restaurants, and petrol is sold more or less over the counter, like brandy. Not the same taste, however. Furthermore, hoteliers in the remoter districts are also very good about selling you a few odd litres here and there. if you get stuck. But it is as well not to let yourself run low in Corsica.

The "name" brands — Esso, Mobilgas, Shell and BP — are all sold, usually without much choice, at these wayside pumps. I was not always sure that what the pump said it sold and what it actually delivered were necessarily one and the same thing, for these outlying pumps are serviced by long-distance lorry and, if the proprietor has a heavy demand on hand, he is unlikely to be fussy. However, petrol connoisseurs can rest assured that the "extra" brands, such as BP Super Plus or Mobilgas Special, are always what they say they are, but they are usually only found in the towns of some size.

Finally, take along with you a spare can of your own oil.

### (iv) *Documents:*

The A.A. and R.A.C. have a well-known and deserved reputation for preparing these for travellers setting out from England. The A.A. and R.A.C. are not exclusive, however, in handling the increasing cross-Channel ferry service; there are several travel agencies that will also look after all these arrangements for you for a small fee.

It is often thought that an international driving licence is essential for continental motoring, but this is no longer the case. Get one if you have time (the R.A.C. handle them), but I have also found that licences of the country of origin are now acceptable in Corsica. But *not* a provisional licence.

If driving a hired Corsican car (*voiture de louage*), you must carry with you at all times not only your own documents but also those furnished for you by the garage, including the police number of the car which, in Corsica, differs from the French registration. One final tip, here. The Corsican sub-number is R 20 and, as there are still relatively few of these vehicles originating on the island, you will be known for what you are, by locals and police alike. At the back of this book I have appended a few French words for important parts of your car. The A.A. has a useful phrase-book of motoring parlance, while both Shell and BP issue booklets designed to help motorists translate technical terms easily.

### (v) *Map:*

No question here. Buy Michelin (obtainable in England from: News Chronicle Book Department, Bouverie Street, London, E.C.4). Michelin is unsurpassed, carries ratings of hotels and restaurants (on which it also publishes separate booklets), insets of major towns, a list of principal curiosities, and so forth. Its scale is 1 cm. to 2 kms. and in general it can't be beaten. Everyone uses it on the island. However, it is a French map and some *caveats* are in order for the Englishman using it.

First of all, Michelin cannot, however hard it tries, keep absolutely up-to-date. Not with Corsican road-makers and breakers, at any rate. I got the most recent edition before my last trip and was still able to find excellent secondary roads entirely unmarked on the map.

Or, take the strip of land jutting out into the sea due east of Porto-Vecchio. Michelin gives it no indicative colouration at all and one would thus surmise it to be arid. In fact, it is a lovely stretch, completely wooded. Further, Michelin accords a blue-green marking to what it considers to be "particularly beautiful forests," unlike the paler, yellower green with which it marks ordinary verdure. But in practice what Michelin means by this accolade is a pine-forest, and whether you think these are beautiful or not is purely opinionative. I happen to prefer by far the leafy chestnut forests in which Corsica abounds, but many of these are not *"particulièrement belle"* according to Michelin. Yet, all things considered, it is the best map to get.

(vi) *Roads:*

As already mentioned, roads alter annually in Corsica. They are only really now recovering from the appalling state they got into during the last war. Their condition is always known to local inhabitants so that, if a waiter or porter happens to tell you of a little track he knows down to a good beach, don't necessarily spurn it because you can't find it on Michelin.

On the other hand, since Michelin seems to my mind to mark as major roads (*routes principales*) those most used, rather than those in the best condition, you may find—as I certainly did—various secondary roads (*routes secondaires*) in far worse condition than some of the tracks (*sentiers*) scarcely dignified with a marking on the map! In other words, an encyclopaedic map such as Michelin cannot in all conscience hope to be comprehensively relative. To name one example: the road into the interior from Solenzara to Zonza, a blindingly beautiful drive up the famous Col de Bavella, was when I took it last a mass of potholes, and shook my little Dauphine to the core. Yet this road is marked as physically on a par with a useful short-cut from Porto-Vecchio just nearby to the Bonifacio-

Sartène road; this drive, which lops off some twenty kilometres should you be in a hurry to reach Ajaccio, and incidentally passes through Sotto and Figari, I found to be about as good as many a minor English road.

My advice, then, is this; road surfaces change rapidly in Corsica. They deteriorate fast, since they are built up fast. If in doubt, check with some local inhabitant, but one who owns a car or uses one. Those who don't — and women — are poor counsel as to what roads are passable, or even in existence, I've found! Waiters seem usually to know the present state of local thoroughfares and, if you plan taking what the French maps tactfully term *une route de viabilité incertaine,* it might be as well to ask one first. A garage mechanic would be even better, but not necessarily a man who sells petrol only; the latter may know absolutely nothing about motoring at all.

By and large, all the principal roads in Corsica are in pretty good order and certainly they make for visually enthralling driving. With the exception of a rather boring stretch in the Middle of the East Coast, it is next to impossible to find an uninteresting road on the island. Characteristically they are cut — laboriously blasted, in fact, year by year — along the sides of the mountains, constantly twisting back on each other, constantly winding (when you see the French hairpin Z sign in Corsica, believe me you're in for a twister!), and the result is that at each curve you seem to find the great gulfs and valleys laid out before you in ever newer and more sharply breathtaking angles. I will take you up some of these shortly.

Let me conclude by saying here that I have heard the coast stretch from Calvi to Porto called the most beautiful road in the world by a seasoned traveller. Although I have myself driven the entire North African stretch from Algiers to Tunis, I am still inclined to agree. Certainly the sections that dominate the leisurely spread of the Girolata and Lignaggia Gulfs give one a sense of driving almost in another element, with the world a whole joyous blue about one.

Naturally enough, however, with this characteristic doubling-back of the Corsican mountain roads, of which no map can give you accurate warning since the bends are so close, there goes a degree of danger. It cannot be emphasized too strongly how important it is in Corsica to — DRIVE CAREFULLY! To this maxim my wife, as the wheels of our Renault teetered over precipitous descents when accosting another car, has more than once warmly added, *If only because no one else seems to!* And I admit her point. The drivers you will encounter are: (a) Corsicans, (b) French tourists, (c) fellow tourists. Of the first group I hope you will meet as few as possible. Corsicans drive as if they owned the road. Which of course they do. And I for one am perfectly content to let them do so. Meeting a set-faced peasant at the wheel of his 1922 Peugeot I am more than happy, at this stage of the game, to draw up, smile politely, and watch him hare ecstatically for the next bend. As to the second category they are usually good and courteous drivers; however, coming from France, they are more familiar with the corniche type of road than we are, and accordingly much more confident.

I might add, by the way, that mutual automobile assistance is a must in Corsica, presumably like the early perambulatory societies when man helped wounded man to limp home through the thorny tracks. If you see someone who has broken down, always pull up and ask if you can help. You may want him to do the same for you one day. And it makes for good ambassadorship into the bargain.

Finally, as regards the category of other tourists, these will mostly be met crawling round the scary bends as slowly as you. They make the least hazard of the lot. A salute of relief is all that is needed as you pass.

In all seriousness, however, the prospective Corsican motorist should perhaps be warned that the most dangerous moment comes when he starts to get the feel of local roads. After a few days of mountain motoring one gets the hang of those corkscrew bends, swings out at the start of each curve and then clings nice and close to the bend from there on in. I would suspect that this moment of *hubris* — automobilistically speaking — is the one of maximum danger. Overconfidence. Guard against it. A blow-out at 50 m.p.h. (80 kms.) would be extremely unpleasant on some of the mountain turns.

In connection with the kind of driving you will find it ncessary to do in Corsica, I might throw out a few further hints from personal experience. First, avoid trying to "make time." Because of the low visibility of the average mountain road on the island, it is hard to develop any speed and you should certainly allow much more time over distances than in England. If you don't, you may find yourself pressing, to reach a certain town before dark, say, or in exasperation at the time taken over a journey marked as just a few kilometres on the map. Every year there are appalling accidents on Corsican roads and I feel sure most of them are caused by drivers trying to beat the clock. Allow yourself, then, easily time and a half what the same distance would take in England, and sit back and enjoy yourself as a consequence. And if you take a bus, relax. Don't do the driving! These bus-drivers are experts and know every inch of the roads.

Secondly, one must obviously change down when navigating the mountain hairpins to save one's over-used brakes, which will soon smell hot if not. The constant narrow bridges, too, cause one to lose all speed before starting the ascent of the other leg of a bend, on many occasions. *Tant mieux* if you have a car that corners well.

If you do not like driving into a low sun, or have no sun-vizor on the car, avoid early morning or late evening driving. The Corsican sun is sharp and bright after about six-thirty, seems to drop fast, and the combination of deep shadow from verdant trees and brilliant sunlight straight in one's eyes can prove most disturbing on the twisty mountain passes. Moreover, it's just impossible to bank on having the sun behind the car because, for instance, one sees from the map that one is travelling eastwards in the evening. Ascending or descending, just as much of the road will wind back into the sun as out of it. Maps simply can't mark all the twists. This advice does not apply to the flat stretch on the east of the island.

One or two small points. Coachwork. If you are keen on yours, watch low projections of rock beneath the driver's eye-level when passing them. These can rip hell out of the body-work and so many of the higher roads are hewn out of overhanging rock. Try to spot them in advance. Also, when parking, leave your car under a tree, allowing for the movement of shadow across it.

Presumably not many visitors will be inclined to drive by night. Should you do so, you will find the roads pleasantly free from traffic. On an eighty-kilometre run just after midnight in the height of the season I met in all two cars coming towards me. This may again induce excessive confidence. Such would be a big mistake. By night Corsican donkeys frequently seek the cozy warmth of roads heated by the day's sun. They lie down and sleep on the tarmac and are extremely difficult to spot until you are right on top of them. Moreover, their front legs are usually tethered so that they can only make short, limping jumps and cannot get out of the way at all quickly, even when warned by the horn. Donkeys (*ânes*) are highly valued for local transportation and a good one costs around 300 N.F. It's even possible to hire them from inhabitants, if you wish. You will see them everywhere you go in Corsica, of course, these quadruped clowns with their tragic eyes rimmed in white.

As one last note, I might say that in my own opinion loose sandals constitute a far greater hazard than driving barefoot, on which police forces frown more overtly. The heavier sandal makes it hard to "heel-and-toe" and is sometimes, when loosely fastened, likely to slip off small pedals.

## CLIMATE

If you have read the foregoing you will understand why I warmly recommend visiting Corsica off-season. The following figures speak for themselves: 29 per cent. of all British tourists go to France and/or its possessions; ten million French leave for their holidays around the middle of July. The majority of these latter are city folk —Paris is estimated to lose up to 70 per cent. of its population through August, present records showing that about a million and a half French leave Paris every ten days by rail alone during the season. More than half of these French holiday-makers take off two weeks to one month. Fifty-one per cent. of all French holidayers choose August, 23 per cent. July.

Note, then, that only a very small percentage of this influential group takes its time off in June or September. Remember that they are used to a warmer climate than ours and so find sea-bathing chillier than we would in those off-season months. But I personally recommend a visit to Corsica in either June or September, if you can

85

at all conveniently manage it. The last June I was there I did not make one reservation in advance and I never once failed to get in where I wanted to. Moreover, for us of the north, the climate is perfect then, the beaches are deserted, and the sea is by no means too cold at all. Neither June nor September are rainy months whereas, when hot spells pile up in August, you often get thunderstorms that hang around for days and knock many expected hours of sunshine off your holiday. And again, if you are really out to see the country, rather than go bathing, May is also excellent. The chart below, (19) which I have translated from the last set of centigrade temperatures registered by M. Jacques, Director of the Station Météorologique d'Ajaccio, shows you how delightfully mild this island of beauty is: one may also observe that June is a slightly warmer month than September.

|  | Average Temperature Fahrenheit | Minimum and Maximum recorded | |
|---|---|---|---|
| JANUARY | 50 | 35.6 | 66.2 |
| FEBRUARY | 42.8 | 39.2 | 62.6 |
| MARCH | 50 | 37.4 | 66.2 |
| APRIL | 54.2 | 32 | 72.1 |
| MAY | 59 | 39.2 | 73.4 |
| JUNE | 68 | 48.2 | 81.9 |
| JULY | 70.1 | 52.7 | 91.4 |
| AUGUST | 71 | 50.5 | 97.3 |
| SEPTEMBER | 65 | 46.4 | 79.4 |
| OCTOBER | 63 | 41 | 79 |
| NOVEMBER | 56.2 | 42 | 71.9 |
| DECEMBER | 49 | 37.4 | 64.4 |

Even with a chart like this, it is extremely hard to characterize the Corsican climate since it is so diverse. Furthermore, it would not be the verdant country it is without a certain rainfall—round about one day out of three in the autumn. After all, in winter, avalanches occur

(19) Compiled over one year.

within forty miles of sunny Ajaccio: let me append another chart, (20) also supplied most kindly by M. Jacques, which demonstrates winter conditions in Ajaccio a little better.

| | Oct. | Nov. | Dec. | Jan. | Feb. | Mar. | Apr. |
|---|---|---|---|---|---|---|---|
| Number of hours of sun .. .. | 210 | 147 | 116 | 125 | 126 | 206 | 231 |
| Average number of days of rain .. | 10 | 13 | 12 | 11 | 10 | 10 | 9 |
| Total hours of rain | 33 | 52 | 56 | 64 | 78 | 46 | 51 |

On the whole, however, it can fairly be taken that the coastal areas have a climate that is pervasively Mediterranean: to which generalization it should be added that the Eastern seaboard has more rain than the Western. At one time the South-Eastern sector of the coastline was malarial but this has now been thoroughly cleared thanks to the efforts, among others, of the U.S. authorities preparing their air base on that side. As a matter of fact, there seem to be particularly few mosquitoes about by night at all.

Then, as noted elsewhere, Corsica suffers strong winds. Its nights, too, can be quite cold, even in June, more especially if one has been motoring and has forgotten just how high one has been climbing. Some sort of heavy jersey or pullover is advised for both sexes. This brings me to the question of clothing.

## CLOTHING

Summer clothing in Corsica is informal in the extreme. The genial Préfet de la Corse, M. Marcel Savreux, is charmingly unassuming in this regard, while women

(20) Compiled over a period of years.

naturally expose as much of themselves to the health-giving rays of the sun as possible; in Bastia business-men leave off their ties, not to be outdone by the sauntering tourist girls for whom a pair of hip-hugging shorts and halter-top are *de rigueur*. Or on the beaches, the inevitable bikini—a bikini, one might add, which looks as if it's been put on with a spray-gun plus a pair of postage stamps, or so-called " pasties," for the top deck.

I labour this point not so much because I am an ardent girl-watcher, as because some of the guide-books to the island are misleading in this respect. I have read of the " black villages," where owing to strict mourning customs nearly everyone is in black, and the women, in particular, clad practically to the toes, their heads swathed in the inky *mezzaro*. These villages (and their customs) are dying out, perhaps unfortunately. Even in the interior the older generation has accepted the light dress of the young of today, just as they have in similar spots in Italy. This is often a relief for English tourists seeking a heavy tan. Dressed in a modest black linen sheath my wife was refused entry into a beach club near Valencia in Spain a year or so ago because she had her shoulders bare—well, not even bare really, but the outfit was sleeveless, to be sure.

It is obviously incumbent on one to respect the customs of the local inhabitants — when in Rome, etc. — but Corsican reserve has been pretty well corrupted as regards clothing by the annual influx of sun-lovers from France. I blinked my eyes on one beach to observe a couple of marrieds playing quoits in shorts only—women included.

No, the French are not inhibited in these matters as we are, and the atmosphere on the beaches they patronize is usually a healthy one, a business of serious sun-tanning and determined exposure. On another stretch of sand I know in Corsica it seemed customary for the ladies in the camping entourage to peel down their already skin-tight bikinis at the back, exposing cleavage at a point where cleavage isn't ordinarily displayed in public. And I didn't hear a single whistle of titillation at one of those rounded rears. In short, have no fear that you'll be lammed into the *juzgado* for indecent exposure in Corsica. The thing's a contradiction in terms. But take it also from me, you'll be hopelessly conspicuous on the beaches there in the kind of overdressed, rubberized corset, which American fashion houses and department stores bemuse their customers into buying, in the idea that "swimsuits are covered-up this year," and the rest of the bunkum.

My advice here is appropriately Napoleonic—to live off the land. Let's face it, for most of us it's rather a compliment to be taken for a native while rubber-necking around some Mediterranean island. The average English print rules this possibility out. To my mind you can always spot an English lady tourist on the continent by : (a) large handbag, (b) flowered print frock, (c) loose, "comfortable" belt, (d) heavy walking sandals. There is nothing against this get-up or rig, of course, but by and large, for protective colouration, I'd advise shorts rather than skirts and possibly some choice of solid colours (though fashions change so quickly this is impossible to prescribe). Let me cite a well-dressed lady on the subject : " Summery prints are a terrible mistake in the big cities like Rome, Paris and London. So are white shoes in the daytime, and white bags." (21)

Plastic fabrics which don't require ironing, such as dacron suits for men and so on, are obviously a con-

---

(21) Dorothy Kilgallen, in *Travel Digest*, September 1958, p. 27.

venience if you are watching your wallet. Hats for men aren't necessary unless you feel the sun particularly acutely. And, indeed, it might be as well to conclude here with a quotation from a fashion arbiter for men, too:

The wise course for the man who travels (and every man travels these days) is to observe Napoleon's campaign rule—to live off the land—by purchasing his accessories locally ... There is nothing more depressing than being branded as a tourist because of the inappropriateness of a shirt or a pair of pants. (22)

## WINTER SPORTS

It has been written that you can have winter and summer combined in Corsica. The double joy of sea and ski-ing. And it is true. You could, if you wanted to, use water and snow skis in a single day there. While bathers tan their flanks on the Ajaccio beaches, you can still (in July) catch sight of runnels of snow on the mountain passes fifty kilometres away. This is the real wonder of Corsica, its amazing variety, and true lovers of nature will discover superior aesthetic qualities about the island in winter, I think.

Two resorts are being developed for winter sports in the interior: these are Vizzavona and Bastelica, the latter in the heart of Sampiero's country. The former is slightly higher, with altitudes varying from 3,000 to 3,770 feet; it has a good run. Bastelica also has an attractive run some four kilometres away on the Ese plateau.

How organized these places are becoming I would not like to say, since I have not personally skied at either. I have, however, read authoritative articles on the skiing

(22) Patrick O'Higgins, " Men's Summer Fashions," *Holiday,* June 1958, p. 150.

available and it would seem at present somewhat limited —a matter of a few hundred enthusiasts partaking each year—but accordingly challenging. Both place are quite lovely, of course. I should imagine prior purchase of equipment would be advisable. Note also that some of the mountain roads are closed by snow in winter. A *coup de téléphone* ahead then, first.


## YACHTING

Again I won't pretend to be an expert. I have merely gone aboard other individuals' vessels and talked cursorily to those who have tied up here and there. But the conditions would seem inviting in the extreme. And naturally you can in this way explore inlets and coves denied to mere mortals with motor-cars.

The West Coast is reputed to be best. There are good anchorages at: Calvi, Porto, Ile Rousse, Cargèse, Ajaccio, Propriano, Bonifacio, Santa Manza, Porto-Vecchio, Bastia, Saint-Florent. The prevailing wind is westerly and an early morning start is recommended, against a stiffening breeze which, while it assists navigation at sea, makes getting off the coast fairly difficult. A reserve of fresh water and a stock of tinned food are advised. As to drink, sailors of this kind are not likely to forget their entitlement to the well-known " out-of-bond " facilities. These, I confess, are about all this landlubber envies them.


## " LE CAMPING "

Not only have the French taken over this term from our language, they have in latter years gone in for this diversion in a far more thorough way than I have ever observed in England. In this the climate is on their side,

91

of course. But here are some interesting figures showing the ratio of campers visiting Corsica annually: (23)

|       | Tourists | Campers |
|-------|----------|---------|
| 1953: | 42,926   | 15,882  |
| 1954: | 58,592   | 16,502  |
| 1955: | 67,319   | 26,700  |
| 1956: | 90,200   | 45,000  |
| 1957: | 106,864  | 65,000  |

The percentage of campers is increasing, and a word or two about what the French call *le camping* is in order for the prospective visitor to the island.

First and foremost, if you are an enthusiast for tented living, let it be said that Corsica is the ideal place for you. All over the countryside, during the crowded holiday months, one can see the dun or green colours of pitched canvas. And the minimum of signs regimenting you this way or that in your choice. Campers in Corsica seem to be able, in fact, to nestle into some of the most delightfully remote and charming nooks imaginable. In the pages that follow I shall try to drop brief hints as to particular spots where conditions are best. They are so very often because a characteristic of many beaches on the island is to have a rivulet of the purest, coldest water imaginable running into them, and one can drink not only with impunity, but with delight, from these erstwhile mountain streams. In summer it is also typical of these streams to be busy gurgles of water all their various paths down to the beaches, only to peter out there, mysteriously enough, in the sand.

---

(23) It is also interesting to observe that until 1958 Anglo-Saxon tourists were in a majority; in 1958 and 1959 the Germans exceeded them, and now the Scandinavian countries are sending more and more. These figures obviously do not include the French.

Owing to the recent French passion for camping, it must not be imagined that this is a poor man's sport. Far from it. Nor even is it the simple preserve of the young. True, I have given lifts to impecunious students on "shoestring" budgets hitch-hiking their way around under postage-stamps of flimsy denim (and, by the way, always give lifts in Corsica). But a large number of campers nowadays will be extremely well-to-do families of the upper middle-class wanting a total break from their city lives on the mainland. A recent issue of a French magazine listed the average age of French campers today as between 45 and 50.

Now the elaboration of effects some of these people bring with them is astonishing. In England we have the car that ingeniously sleeps two on top and so forth, but my wife and I really blinked our eyes on one plage in Corsica, where a zippered tent of a delicate shade of baby-blue was raised on an outside aluminium frame (treated to deflect heat) in a matter of minutes by remote push-button control from a nearby car. On later inspection, and invitation, it turned out that the family in question had provided themselves with fluorescent light fixtures, shiny stove and sink (running hot and cold water), a radio powered by the sun, and an underwater scooter (for towing lung-divers about). Twentieth-century camping, indeed. And it is said that the Germans have it even better laid on.

Gone are the days of poles and guy-ropes. Instead, something resembling a closed-in 15-cwt. truck is now *de rigueur*, or a heavy Citroën bristling with outlets for electrically heated sleeping bags, frying pans, and the like. In brief, *" le camping n'est plus un jeu."* But the golden rule for anyone intending to camp in Corsica, from the owners of gin-palaces such as those I've described down to the humblest student in his flea-bag beneath the stars, is this: ALERTE AU FEU!

Corsica's two greatest enemies today are forest fires, fanned by strong winds. This is something really serious for the country, and care in this respect cannot be over-emphasized. If you have children, be lynx-like over them here. All summer long you will see small *maquis* fires, here and there, but for an example of what truly dreadful devastation forest fires can wreak in Corsica I recommend a glance as you go by at the (sometime) Forêt d'Esigna, south-east of Piana. I must have motored this road dozens of times and, for anyone who loves natural beauty, the sight of those blackened hillsides and writhing tree-stumps is an absolute agony.

This is not a book on camping, any more than it is on European motoring, and I do not propose to take up a lot of space on advice as to what or what not to take on such a holiday. (24) French families frequently arrive with small lorry-loads of such stuff. In any case, enthusiasts will know far better than me how to provision themselves for such expeditions. Big shops, like the Army and Navy in London, now run whole departments to advise you in such matters. Suffice it to say here that there are places in Corsica where you can and places where you cannot camp. The latter are plainly marked. The former are often indicated by the notice, LICENCE DE CAMPER. This means, inquire first at the local town Mayor's (Mairie); better still, if you plan to camp at all in Corsica, pick up an authorization (free) from the *Conservateur des Eaux et Forêts* in Ajaccio. If you are in open

---

(24) S. B. Hough's *A Pound A Day Inclusive* has an excellent appendix on what to take camping, while the annual *Camping en France* can keep you up to date on local conditions and requirements.

forest country, and can't see a *Mairie,* enquire for the local gamekeeper, or *garde-forestier.* Beware, however, of camping in chestnut groves, where insects abound. Plages are generally an open market. But not always.

The easiest, and probably most satisfactory, method, particularly from the point of view of availability of water and supplies, is to rent space from one of the several *camping* establishments that have lately mushroomed all over the island. This can be done very cheaply—sometimes almost literally for a song; and here it is I touch on that other aspect of this vexed subject, namely what the French often refer to as *le camping* when making recommendations for accommodation, places where, in fact, you may not find a speck of canvas in sight.

For as a consequence of having turned into a Mecca for campers, Corsica has sprouted a large number of jerry-built collections of cabins, shacks, sheds, benches, bamboo enclosures, and barren-looking plaster or log bungalows (usually given exotic names) designed by some *camping* association or club to house as many groups of open-air enthusiasts as possible during the season. You will soon see the signs: Club Olympique de Paris, Club Mediter-ranée, Club Franco-Britannique, Club des Eclaireurs de France, Club Hollandais, Club des Amis de la Nature, Club Uncle Tom Cobley and All. Germans, Danes, Swedes, Dutch, and Austrians are all now getting into the act. There seems no stop to it at all. (What happens when the Russians, and Chinese, are allowed to travel?) *Le camping* grows annually.

The usual configurations these campings assume — and they are invariably close to the sea — is a litter of the most primitive sheds imaginable, generally knocked up by the proprietor and his wife and friends, who have most likely pitched in their little all for the necessary land. There will be an Army-style cookhouse, a barrack for the *personnel*, or staff, a communal mess-room with shared tables *al fresco*, and latrines and washing accommodation to match. When you put one of these establishments, as one club has just outside Ajaccio, in between two characteristically opulent Corsican cemeteries, (25) the end result looks wildly surrealist.

After they have been going a year or so, these places next burgeon an almost studiedly hideous stretch of cement (surrounded by second-hand chairs) on which to cha-cha. This is labelled a Bar-Dancing, and is considered an attraction by night. Perhaps I had too much of this sort of set-up, or its near-neighbour, the tented Army camp, given me gratis in North Africa during the war, for me to be able to speak objectively, or even civilly, about *le camping*. Let me try to be tolerably fair, however.

Now I have actually put up at a number of these establishments and have invariably found the managements to be without exception delightfully friendly and courteous. They are nearly always people who like doing this sort of thing, and in summer months swell their staff with French students, who can be very good fun indeed. There is all the difference in the world between a band that labours wearily through the night for cash and a group of energetic enthusiasts who play (and often play extremely well) solely for the love of it, plus a buckshee holiday in the sun.

For a few days, then, if you are prepared to rough it as regards washing arrangements (and are you, O senior reader of this book, on your one holiday of the year?), these places can be worth while. As often as not they are

(25) Corsica has the finest graveyards in the world. Local families sometimes put all their savings into vaults.

Cargèse: showing the two churches, Greek and Roman
Catholic, which dominate the village.

6.                       Coming down to Porto from Piana.

7.          Porto: the Marine and the peaks of Poglia-Orba.

in glorious situations, close to the countryside rather than the town, and the feeling of being "away-from-it-all" you get for the first few days of such open-air life is a terrific tonic. Certainly wonderful for children (some campings run a compulsory silence at 22.00 on certain nights of the week for their benefit). As I say, then, worth a try for a while if you're travelling round and are likely to strike one of the better hotels shortly afterwards for the sake of the amenities.

All the same, as an *"ami de la nature"* myself, I am afraid I find these phenomena a menace. I envisage every beach in Corsica being in the lap of some *camping* or other in ten years' time; and, as not all the managers concerned, however personally courteous, are either interested in preserving the indigenous character of Corsica or have much taste at all, they seem to me — with notable exceptions — to be systematically ruining some of the finest landscape in the world.

Sooner or later, it strikes me, a decision will have to be taken concerning *le camping*. I hope it will be the right one and that the vulgarians among these entrepreneurs will be curbed.

Still, one cannot put the clock back even if one wants to and in all good conscience it should be added that *le camping* provides remarkably cheap holidays for people, young people in particular, who might never otherwise get abroad at all. For next to nothing these camps do offer a wonderfully healthy outdoor life and can be warmly recommended, the better ones, to our own youth seeking a holiday both in the Mediterranean and amongst other nationals — nearly all the clubs that organize these places are wide open to any European who wishes to apply. Such a holiday would certainly be a first-class way of improving one's French.

97

Parenthetically, I say the better clubs because they vary in reputation, and I have certainly not tested anything like all of them. I shall draw attention below to one or two I stayed at personally and which I can recommend. But how well or ill earned was the rumour of "smiles of a summer night" in some of the camps must remain — alas? — a mystery. Most of them, in passing, looked the height of respectability, barring, if you will, the succinct bikinis that the French misses wear there on almost every occasion.

Once again, for further information, consult your travel agent or "Essitac." The Union Française des Associations de Camping (22 Avenue Victoria, Paris 1) is the headquarters of these clubs, whose names may also readily be found in the French *Guide Camping* (available from: Editions Susse, 13 Rue de Grenelle, Paris 7). Reservations during July and August are essential at these camps — at least, if you want to sleep in the regulation *bungalow* (the French again use our word for it). I don't, however, think you will find much difficulty hiring tent space at any time.

All in all, *le camping* is opening the gate to the desecration of Corsican landscape. It is far more noxious to natural beauty than road-building, which is extremely hard on this island, thanks to the mountains. When, as once happened to me, you watch no less than five hundred bodies descend en masse on a tiny *camping* already bursting its buttons by holding some two hundred, you realize there are just too many people for the organizations involved, each being roughly the size of a normal Army company. Even if these tourists had come with the best intentions in the world, which most had not (simply approaching Corsica as a bathing beach), they could not help but transform the quiet little valleys and woods they proceeded to inundate. In this case a rush was made for the Bar-Dancing, another for the plage, a third for the *pedalos* (pedal-boats for two hirable at nearly all these establishments). Screams of joy punctuated the steady drone of the motor-boat tugging tense water-skiers, while customers lined up and jostled for position ten deep on a raft for the next ride. If this was Corsica, they seemed collectively to express, it was for them! But if organized volley-ball, ping-pong marathons, megaphone announcements, and queueing up for Cokes do not particularly appeal to you, avoid *le camping* like the plague.

## BEACHES — BATHING AND SWIMMING

One of the French Government guides I have lists Corsican beaches with an *x* to indicate fine sand and an *o* to mark a mixture of fine sand and shingle (*gravillon*). This can be misleading because the state of the sand on Mediterranean beaches depends so much on recent storms and seas. There is a charmingly sandy little plage to be found as you drive northwards out of Saint-Florent, but when I went back to it not long ago, it was almost unrecognizable; high tides and heavy seas had piled weed up until no sand was visible at all. A shame.

On the whole, however, Corsica is unusually blessed with sand beaches, far more so than crowded Italy or the south of France, for instance. Moreover, these vary to suit all tastes. If you are an ardent swimmer, you will find shores that drop steeply into the sea; if, on the other hand, you don't swim or have children who can't, there are several beaches, similar to the famous one at Calvi, which shelve so gently that it is literally a long walk to get out of your depth! With one or two well-known exceptions, these waters are as safe for bathers as most Mediterranean beaches are. If in any doubt about this, ask for some local information on currents (*courants*) at your hotel.

And the delightful thing is, once again, the variety of the sand in Corsica. Not only does it vary in texture, from the silken smooth to the toughly gritty, its colour alters too, from the platinum of the Porto-Vecchio area to the yellow of the West coast, to, finally a strange eerie blue around Nonza in Cap Corse.

Lastly — may I beg you *not to litter* these beaches.

It is so easy not to, and it is really so beastly coming up from some dive into a brilliant blue sea to find someone's old cigar-butt or plastic bag floating inches off one's nose.

## FISHING

Sea fishing is everywhere first-class. All the usual Mediterranean species can be found off the Corsican coasts, including tunny, sardine, conger-eels of great length, mullet (*muzzari,* locally), devil fish, sea-bream, so on. Lobsters can be located chiefly along the West coast and indeed this coastline, which shelves steeply into the sea, is most interesting for the submarine fisherman. If you do like what the French call *la pêche sous-marine,* however, I urge you to buy your equipment — masks, spears, fins — before arrival. There are shops in Ajaccio and Bastia selling these items, naturally enough, but the material is not always of the best. Frankly, I buy mine in Italy.

Fresh-water fishing can be had either in the mountain streams or the ponds dotted along the Eastern seaboard. Trout fishing is authorized from February to October and during the season you can also find shad in these streams. If you are planning to do some fairly earnest river fishing, however, you should apply for a licence therefor to: M. Antoine Villanova, Trésorier de la Fédération de Pêche et de Pisciculture, 55, Cours Napoléon, Ajaccio. Alternatively to: M. Boyer, 11, Avenue Carnot, Bastia.

Finally, if you want to learn how to use an aqua-lung, at least one camp I know conducts daily summer classes in this — the Club Mediterranée in the Golfe de Santa Giulia south of Porto-Vecchio.

## FOOD AND DRINK

On my first visit to Corsica I was warned that I should find the cooking poor. As my first two meals on the island were had at the Concorde, in Bastia, and the Côte d'Azur, in Ajaccio, I began to think. What had actually happened had been that I'd simply eaten at two of the best restaurants there. In both the cooking is superlative, of the first quality by any standards. This also applies to the admirable cuisine at the Hôtel Napoléon-Bonaparte at Ile Rousse. As so it should for such an establishment.

The point is: What are you judging by? Corsica is French, and French cooking is, in my humble opinion, mouth-watering. It seems impossible to find a bad restaurant in Paris, for example. Thus French guide-books will be found in this instance to be conservative in their gastronomic recommendations. Writing for an English public I prefer to go out on a limb — as our transatlantic cousins put it. First, let me assert that there is considerably less strain on the British stomach imposed by Corsican, rather than by, say, Italian cooking. Intestinal adjustments are likely to be negligible.

Frankly, coming from England, the cuisine at the better restaurants in Ajaccio and Bastia, as listed variously below, tastes perfectly wonderful. It is less good at the average hotel (I have indicated exceptions to this rule as I go along), descending to the definitely poor in roadside inns and hostelries. How many times have I been lured

101

into stopping at some wayside pub, charmingly situated, tranquil and cosy-looking, only to be sadly disappointed by the diet provided. This does tend to get monotonous throughout. Hotel fare usually does, in any case. And I am afraid one has to admit that that feeling of real interest in food one finds everywhere in France is somewhat lacking in Corsica. Somewhat.

It is, of course, a prime heresy to say this, just as it is to tell an Italian that the celebrated Cucina Toscana is dull and reasonably unimaginative after a while, or that, with the exception of a few wines produced above Verona, Italian wines are fairly indifferent, that the famous Frascati of which Romans boast is, in the words of a candid Frenchman, second-class cider. Let me say that I have read pages of eulogy on Corsican cooking, and if you want to get this really hot and strong, buy *La Gastronomie Corse* by Simone Costantini. (26) At the same time, the incomparable Costantini knows the situation all right. Let me quote:

Culinary tradition is being blunted by the *brouhaha* of contemporary chaos and thus the secrets of traditional dishes are losing their ties with life. They are being replaced, more and more each day, by the *Ersatz* of habituation to the impersonal and hurried cooking of the city, without any local colour and of a sad uniformity. (27).

Nor are prices cheap in Corsica. In France wayside taverns will serve delicious meals for much less than you pay in Paris. Naturally, you say. But such is far from the

(26) With a Preface by the renowned Curnonsky; privately printed and available from: Mme. S. Costantini, Maison Bellevue, Ghisoni, Corse.

(27) From a preface to the programme of a Grand Bal for the Association Corse, held 16 March, 1957; my translation.

case in Corsica. The set luncheon when I was last at the Concorde in Bastia was a four-course affair costing six New Francs. At a scruffy little inn at Sagone I paid eight for an incredibly inferior meal. Why? Because, so the shrugged reply runs, they have transport costs to pay at such places, they have to fetch and carry their food from the big centres. A dubious excuse!

Always examine the menu first; this is usually on display outside the restaurant or dining-room. Everyone does this. The set meal is printed on one side, often enough, and the A la Carte offerings on the other. Don't forget that in Corsica if you order *"un menu,"* it means that you want one set lunch, please; whereas the phrase most current for something A la carte is to ask for a dish *"sur commande."*

Nobody is out to swindle you in Corsica—except perhaps the few palpable brigands at tourist havens like Porto or Propriano — and you will invariably get good value for your money as regards food. The common exception to this is *le picnic*. The average basket luncheon (*panier*) an hotel will make up for you for a day on the beach is not worth the 5 N.F. or so. I always prefer to buy some ham and fruit and stuff in a local *Epicerie,* or grocers, instead.

Set meals presently run, then, between 6 and 10 N.F. without wine and any extras. In general, food is not cheap, nor is it exceptionally expensive. It is rare to get a very large bill for any meal in Corsica.

Now, as to what one eats. Alas, except for those few enlightened restaurants scattered about, the average hotelier on the island is getting a more and more limited impression of "what the tourist wants." After Bastille Day (14th July) the French start streaming down to Corsica by car, bawling for *langouste*. (28) Very well, say the hoteliers, let them have *langouste;* and there are usually plenty on hand, as expensively priced as they dare. There is also *le bifsteck,* too, and a rote of poultry and hors d'oeuvres. I might add that the only *escargots* I got on the island tasted excellent, but they were preserved ones — I have eaten *fresh* snails, straight from a soaking in their tubs, in a cheap French restaurant in New York.

But I suggest it is a considerable tragedy if the standardization of daily life becomes such in our industrialized civilization that it effects our palates, also. This is just what has happened in the hinterland of America, of course, where Momma, Poppa, and Junior all whale into their hamburger and franks for meal after meal. *Langouste* is good. But so are shrimps, crabs, and other shell-fish which now seldom put in an appearance before their ubiquitous senior brother. (Local eels are noted, too, but who has seen them?)

What I am getting at is what I have found from sad experience to be the case in Corsica, namely that the A la Carte listings one sees there, exotic as they appear in print, bear decreasing resemblance to what is actually in stock in the kitchen. After my wife and I had stayed in an hotel for any length of time it became quite habitual, in fact, for the A la Carte menu to be riddled with crossed-off dishes, which no one had thought of ordering for years, so it seemed. Thus, Porto-Vecchio is reputed to be famous for the succulence of its *coquilles,* those giant mussels, or clams, which stick straight up in the sea and contain such a tasty morsel of fish-meat. But if you can get *coquilles*

(28) Technically, *langouste* is *langouste.* Lobster, with the large claws, is *homard* and generally has to be especially ordered; it tastes better, in my opinion. I have appended a brief glossary of menu terms at the back of this book.

served to you in Porto-Vecchio you're a better man than I am, Gunga Din. You either have to dive for the darned things yourself or practically buy a boatman to pick them for you.

I speak with feeling on this subject since my wife happens to be an enthusiastic cook and is stubborn about getting served with recherché dishes not in the general order of the day. (Ah, those moments when the waiter's pencil flies, and I feel surreptitiously for my wallet to do some more amateur trigonometry with the banknotes there). The first time we went to Corsica we provided ourselves with a glowing brochure from the French Government Tourist Agency describing, in unbearably realistic terms, the delicacies of the Corsican cuisine. You too may acquire this little pamphlet, if you wish. Its interest, I wager, will remain mainly academic unless, of course, you go in the late autumn or early winter. Another good reason, incidentally, for an off-season visit.

Having said as much, and been as dismayingly honest as I must, let me in fairness add that Corsica is rightly renowned for certain regional delicacies. (29) At the beginning of the century it looked as if the island might develop into a resort for the *haut monde*. Edward VII went there and explicitly preferred Ajaccio to Naples, the Archduke Charles of Austria wintered there then, as well as many other leaders of fashion. But the first world war altered the current of this clientele to the South of France, where a number of disused mansions were made over into luxury hotels and where, as we all well know, the clientele of this kind has stayed. Ajaccio actually lost six hotels in a short time during this period.

---

(29) For an English account of a most elaborate meal, see: Evan Jones, " Corsica—The Scent of Thyme," *Harper's Bazaar,* June, 1958.

105

But at the height of its popularity among the rich Corsica offered a number of national dishes which today, because of the lack of sensitive demand, become annually rarer, or at least harder to obtain. *Caprettu,* young roast kid grazed on *maquis,* and available only in spring, is thus getting rarer and rarer. It is merely another tragedy of our times.

Naturally those living on the island all year round can get what they like of seasonal dishes, particularly if they have plenty of servants. Not so we summer visitors. And as if to mock us, we are greeted at every restaurant with the invitation: SPECIALITES CORSES. It is one of the most frequently seen signs about.

What are these Corsican specialities? *"Une énumération complète serait fastidieuse,"* replies Costantini, who gives a vast list. But let me limit myself to experience, mainly of summer dishes. These I propose to take in their order of appearance in the meal.

*Charcuterie Corse.* The most common of all Corsican foods at table. Literally, any pig product. In practice, in the hors d'oeuvres position, anticipate a selection of salami sausage and smoked ham (*lonzo* or *lonzu*) and prosciutto. The last (*prisuttu*) is rawer and cruder in taste than the Italian varieties. *Salticcio* resembles the peppery Italian capricolla.

*Pâtés. Terrine* or *pâté de merles* (blackbirds) or of *grives* (thrushes). The former is more common since the blackbird comes slightly fatter in Corsica. Don't miss these creamy potted meats. They are very delicious if the birds have been allowed to *mortifier* well, as the French put it, without being cleaned first. Such small birds roast are also excellent, if you like a gamy meat. The local rabbits here generally disappoint.

*Huîtres*. In season first-class oysters from the Etang de Diana, half-way down the East Coast, may be eaten.

*Suppa de faggioli rossi*. There are many superb French soups, of course; this is an excellent one made with the local red beans (*haricots rouges*) of the type used in the common cassoulet.

*Truite*. Corsican trout is highly touted. The pearl of the island's gastronomy, according to Costantini. I have tried it in several places, including the Evisa district renowned for it, but frankly I didn't find it a patch on Dublin sea-trout. But I may have been unlucky.

*Bouillabaisse* (or *uziminu*). Can be extremely tasty if done well, at a good fish place. Always plentiful, in fact perhaps too much of a good thing sometimes, so order sparingly with it.

*Cheeses*. Absolutely first-class. From both goat and sheep. The Venaco and Niolo cheeses excel. There is a very strong local variety called *broccio* or *brocciù*. (30) And don't forget that the French cheeses, like the ever-delectable Port Salut, are always in good supply and come very cheap.

*Cakes*. Traditionally simple, but good. Sometime, somewhere or other, you are almost bound to be served with *fiadone* (again, variously spelt), a plain but pleasant cheese-cake which goes well with one's coffee. There are other cakes made with chestnut flour, which are rarer. Probably all sent to Nice.

The above, then, are the principal *Specialités Corses* you will be most likely to run into. I have deliberately refrained

---

(30) These Corse names vary in spelling. Corsican orthography is not always conventionalized, at least not against the improvisations of restaurateurs! The strong *u* sound at the end of these words represents the way they are pronounced, even if spelt with an *o*. The daily greeting between Corsicans, which comes from this vowel sound, seems at first like a grunt of pain!

from listing others (the roe of sea urchin, and so on) which would show research on my part, but little else. Local honey (*miel*), pleasantly scented from the *maquis,* is excellent and may be bought in the shops. Again, you don't see it too often on the hotel menus. Zonza is the honey headquarters, and we tried and tried . . .

Another exciting item you will not find in summer is the *bécasse,* or woodcock with the beak of a snipe. These are becoming rarer on the table even in autumn now. But anywhere you walk through waist-high *maquis* you will be bound to start several of these lovely birds, as well as Corsican partridge, and send them whirring on their way. I must have flushed dozens in my day but the discriminating gourmet, from whom these birds tear cries of joy at the table, should employ a gamekeeper. Corsicans go after them less and less.

The trouble is that where there is no demand the Corsican is not going to bother to bestir himself to create it. My own suspicion is that fish and fowl abound in a sportsman's paradise in Corsica, but less and less of it is getting to the cookhouse each year.

As for drink: Corsica produces a number of fine, strong wines. The most famous name in this field is Mattei, and the best-known vineyards those of Molino-Bianco, Patrimonio, and Porretone. Thus some of the brands you will be able to choose from will be: Patrimonio, Royal Corse (the name, incidentally, of the first Corsican regiment), Fleur de Maquis, Malvoisie, Laetizia, and others.

I do not pretend to be a connoisseur but I have drunk wine with my meals most of my life and, on this basis and this only, I make the following recommendations: Patrimonio red wine — like a full-bodied claret; Laetizia white wine — a dry sauterne; Royal Corse rosé.

Corsica is noted for its rosé wines and, as far as I am concerned, quite correctly so. They look like red ink but they are wonderful when served well chilled — though beware of the waiter who seems to imagine that one automatically wants ice in any beverage, including red wine. (The red wines should be drunk *chambré,* "roomed," i.e. at room temperature). The Royal Corse rosé is, to my mind, quite superior and not at all expensive by English standards. Yet, all the rosées are good.

Corsica is finally famous for two liqueurs you will have no difficulty coming by at all: namely, Cédratine and Myrte. The first, a yellowish liquid, is made with the co-operation of the *cédratier,* or Corsican lemon-tree, and the second from the myrtle. Both are good, but neither is really any cheaper, surprisingly enough, than the great French liqueurs you can get on the island also. Try to get a sip of a local brandy, found in country districts, an *eau-de-vie* laced with *Myrte.*

Unlike North Africa, Corsica does not make its own pre-meal apéritif, unless you really enjoy a sticky glass of *muscat* before eating. *Pastis* (varieties of Pernod, with a strong aniseed or licorice flavour) are much drunk by the locals, though not dropped over sugar, as so often in Spain; also *menthe à l'eau,* a mint drink to which water is added, seems popular. Both are acquired tastes, and possibly tastes you may not want to acquire.

Apéritifs depend on your personal predilections more than anything, perhaps. The French themselves continue to favour the sweet vermouths, the Saint-Raphaëls and Byrrhs, before their evening degustation. These you will find easily enough. The Italian bitter apéritifs are also obtainable, though less common, and don't forget in this connection that if you ask for a martini, you will receive a vermouth. Sherry is scarce and gins and whiskies are costly. It should perhaps be added here that Corsica once enjoyed certain tax exemptions on tobacco and alcohol, but as regards the latter there is now virtually no difference between local and French prices — with the exception of local *marc,* or brandy spirit, which can be bought for around seven bob a quart. There is, however, a cigarette factory on the island and if you can smoke French cigarettes, you will find the local *Mistrals* cheaper than like brands sold on *le continent*.

Every kind of soft drink abounds. This includes the famous, or infamous, Coca-Cola, Pepsi, and Seven-Up. Note that in this field a *citronade* differs from a *limonade,* although both will come bottled and fizzy (*pétillant*). If you want a fresh lemon drink squeezed out for you, ask for a *citron pressé*. The latter word in this context has nothing to do, as it usually has, with being hurried.

Water is drinkable (*potable*) in nearly all hotel rooms. When it is not, it is generally marked as such. Do not be afraid to ask first, if you feel like it, however.

To conclude, let me warmly recommend for its digestive properties the famed mineral water (*eau minérale*) called Orezza, from the springs of that name in the Castagniccia. You can buy all the best French brands, too, of course, but Orezza is deservedly well-known and Corsicans always seemed pleased when you prefer it. If you are hitting the bottle in any sort or manner, one of these alkaline mineral waters with your meals is a must. As observed, Corsican wines are potent, and hangovers accordingly heavy. Orezza is sold in both large and small sizes; for the latter, ask the waiter for a *quart* (this does not mean two pints).

## TIPPING

Let me say straight away that never once in Corsica have I known anyone so much as look at a tip, let alone

110

question its amount. Only in the over-touricized resorts, such as Calvi, Propriano, or Porto, may be found those notices outside bars reminding foreigners that service is not *compris,* or included (and I fear it often isn't, when I see such). But then, these places are spoken of with contempt by inhabitants of the interior.

Only once did I have a tip returned to me, and that was a proper rejoinder to a piece of social clumsiness on my part. I had driven down a suicidal mule-track which continually narrowed till my Dauphine seemed to be sprouting roots, down towards an irresistible fingernail of sand I had spotted (such a peerless and inaccessible spot I refuse to divulge its whereabouts)—when I came up against a gate. Doubting that I could open it and go through into what seemed pretty obviously private pro-perty, I got out and walked a couple of fields to where a singing labourer was stooking hay on to one of these charming round stacks with a stake in the middle, to be found in both Italy and Corsica. By what seemed to me a fantastic coincidence, though after a while one con-stantly comes across the same faces in Corsica, this farm labourer was a fellow I had met in another part of the island, where he had performed an unrequited service for me. He at once interrupted both his work and his delight-fully lugubrious Corsican chant to come running all the way back, wring my hand, open the gate for my car. He then conducted me personally across several fields, over a stile, through a stream (removal of shoes, etc.).

This, I considered, deserved some reward and as we parted I pressed a franc on him. It was returned to me. As so it should have been. But the good fellow's treatment of my *gaffe* was in marked contrast to that of a Mexican taxi-driver years ago; this citizen inspected the fairly lavish gratuity I'd given him as if the coins might

111

have been infected, then tossed them to a group of urchins playing nearby, making certain, of course, that I didn't miss the gesture, nor the jet of darkly aimed saliva that succeeded it. ($64,000 question: how far did that chap's pride go? Did he collect the money from the kids again directly I was out of sight?)

Overtipping, meanwhile, is another vulgarity not likely to be indulged in by our countrymen. All the same, a brief warning against it is conceivably due, since in Corsica the sense of aristocratic pride is such that it would be especially offensive there.

Now part of the hokum of travel articles in glossy magazines, of pamphlets issued by banks, travel brochures, and so on, is to encourage you to tip not wisely but too well, simply because of course such sources want the employees involved in this shake-down kept happy. One can always smell out a vested interest, but even so some of the recommendations in this regard I have seen lately have been truly savage.

"Tipping on steamships has almost a recognized standard rate," I read in an American travel guide before me, which goes on to set out a system of tipping table, bedroom, desk, and bathroom stewards on board which altogether tots up to some twenty-five per cent of the total transatlantic fare! Another article in an American fashion monthly recently reiterates this "recognized standard rate," which, believe me, is absolute hooey, and certainly not recognized by the large majority of passengers travelling. I have crossed the Atlantic a number of times, in all classes, and know just how phoney these figures can be.

Parenthetically, one might add that the celebrated saying about owning a Rolls-Royce applies here — if you want to know how much it costs to run one, then you have no

8.                     The Gulf of Girolata.


9.                     Calvi harbour.

10. Calvi: a typical Corsican street scene.

11. Calvi: the church of Sainte-Marie-Majeure.

12.                                       Calvi: the Citadelle.

13.                 Montemaggiore: a typical terraced hill village in the Balagne
behind Calvi.

14.          Saint-Florent: the fishermen's harbour.

15.                    The Convent of Pino.

business to be buying one in the first place. Precisely. If you want to match money with the "happy few" who have to live at this rate, choose better values for your money. In Corsica, at any rate, overtipping would be tactless, to say the least.

On the whole, then, the *pourboire* is gratefully received there, as an acknowledgment of personal service. Glancing through the hotel bills I have, I would say that when Corsican hotels do charge for service it is usually at a rate of 12—15 per cent. Or more. Depending on kitchen arithmetic, which should of course be watched. In this case, a minimum tip for table and room service is all that's needed. Say 5 or 6 per cent all round. On the other hand, I have several bills, generally from the nicer places, with no service charge at all added; in these cases I dispensed some 10 per cent (exclusive of bar charges) among table and room staff and it was happily received. The principle I have here always applied with satisfactory results has been one derived from travel in Italy: *viz.,* give a little to a lot of people, rather than a lot to one single individual. Don't forget that porters in France, as in America, have a tariff per item carried—usually 50 centimes per piece of baggage. Simply ask them. In fact, one really need not worry about tipping at all, you know.

For tipping is rapidly becoming so standardized throughout Europe that advice about it is largely redundant. I have, however, found that because of the history of our currency hardships after the war the British have acquired an ill-merited reputation for being stingy in this way. It seems to me imperative to break down this idea and I feel certain that your holiday will be a far more relaxed one if you inwardly determine from the start that part of it will include that feeling of pleasant self-indulgence which belongs to being more lavish than usual. Remember Scrooge!

At the same time, there are conventions as regards tipping that apply in Corsica, as in France. Tips are given, for instance, to cinema and lavatory attendants, and to the waiter who brings you your drink at a café table. When you take a stand-up drink at a bar this is not required, but there is generally a small plate or other receptacle into which it is polite to slip 3 or 4 per cent of the price of your libation. Frankly, it has always seemed to me fairly fantastic to tip a barman for reaching up his arm and pouring from a bottle, for, in other words, doing no more than his job, but it is done and that's that. It's done wildly in America. I have seen a gum-chewing lothario with Renaissance sideburns behind a bar in a New York night-spot pocket a dollar bill for a round of drinks costing less than five times as much without a murmur of thanks. In Corsica at least you will be thanked. And don't, by the way, be Anglo-Saxonly inhibited about clapping your hands for service; this gesture seems feudal to many, but it's the recognized way of getting a waiter.


## SHOPPING (31)

Just after the last war it was possible to pick up wonderful bargains in various European countries. This day is over now, and I predict that it will remain so unless something like a war should once again cast up artificial economic barriers between nations.

With the spread of an homogeneous technology over Europe in the past decade, prices have become more and more standardized. Machine-made goods cost very roughly

---

(31) Corsicans sternly observe the afternoon siesta, and morning shopping hours end at midday in most places.

the same in this country or that. I once worked out with my wife the relative prices of a raftful of summer clothes she had collected — shorts, and so on — in five different European countries we had visited *and* America. By and large they all tallied. There were no bargains. American prices, for women's clothing at any rate, were not high.

Corsica has not become so rapidly mechanized as, say, its neighbour Italy and one might expect to find a plethora of attractively hand-made goods there at rock-bottom prices. Such is not the case, I fear. Don't expect to be tempted by its shops, as you were by Florence shops. Imported French commodities may even sell for more than in France. And there is everywhere in Corsica the kind of shop that sells allegedly hand-made gimcrackery — carved wood ashtrays, penknives, pipes, shell necklaces, ear-rings, so forth. Apart from their dubious sentimental interest as souvenirs, these monstrosities are a total waste of money, in my opinion, and can be found (St. Ives subbing for Calvi, say) in English tourist resorts when you get back. These shops are evidently somebody's idea of "what the tourist wants" and personally I think they should be discouraged. They usually stock good collections of postcards of the island, however (25 centimes for black and white, and 40-50 centimes for colour).

After which gloomy prognosis, let me assure you that in Bastia, Ajaccio, and Calvi the shops have everything you want. The chemists' emporiums are excellent in this respect, and you need have no fear of not finding things like film, (32) health salts, Bandaid, your favourite brand of lipstick, soap, sanitary napkins, and all the rest. Contraceptives require a doctor's prescription.

---

(32) Very rough film rating conversion advice is appended at the back of this book.

Characteristically fine French bookshops abound in Ajaccio and Bastia, and some of these stock British pocket books. Incidentally, a large number of newsagents on the island carry London newspapers on the day after publication. (There are a host of small Corsican news-sheets, but I won't bother to enumerate them here since they print such purely local gossip; there is a good Corsican page, and Corsican advertisements, in the daily French *Nice-Matin*).

The best buys, then, are undoubtedly, as in France, in the field of perfume and liquor. And cheeses. You can get every kind of leading French perfume in Bastia and Ajaccio, but if you do load up with this kind of wife-pacifier do see that it is well packed. Else it can play havoc with adjacent clothing. Local liqueurs — such as the Cédratine and Myrte mentioned — are really cheap by English standards, well under half their price at home in many cases. Good savings can also be effected by buying the "name" French brands, but again — pack carefully. You would be insane to buy whisky in Corsica, of course, but you might care to bring back some local wines you've particularly enjoyed. Champagnes are expensive since they all come from France. British Customs officials always allow a few bottles through, if directly declared. Check the obtaining regulations as to amounts before leaving.

Beyond this, I have few recommendations. There is the man's *basco* beret to buy, the neat French kind, that is, not the British Army type. For the ladies there are quite good local sandals (33) and French bikini bathing-costumes; becoming examples of the latter are not always

---

(33) Rope-soled *espadrilles*, or canvas shoes, look and feel nice in the Mediterranean area, but they wear out rapidly.

easy to pick up in London. Bring a spare British bathing-cap, however. Useful under showers, too.

For both men and women I recommend the gaily striped sailor's shirts much worn about the island. Try to buy these, though, in the sort of shop a local fisherman would patronize, rather than in the chic boutiques, and you'll get a good buy. What's more, wearing something like this you tend to fade into the wall-paper more, as the expression goes. The white striped vests sailors buy here are most attractive and, being of a loosish weave, seem to keep one warm when it's cold and cool when it's warm. Then, if you are really enterprising, and have a taste for interior decoration, you could probably pick up in local shops interesting and evocative items such as lobster pots (for wastepaper baskets) and continental door-number discs.

Finally, let me add that as you are required to declare your purchases on return, it is convenient to keep a list of these separately, to which you can add as you go along. Keep this with your passport.

## TAXIS

Avoid them. In my experience, and it may perhaps have been an unhappy one in this regard, taxis in Corsica are exorbitantly expensive. They are, in fact, the only item of one's holiday to be so. At a rough computation I have found them to be about double London rates, and we hear enough complaints about those at home! For instance, I was recently charged 5 N.F. from the new port in Bastia to the Ile de Beauté hotel there, a grand drive of possibly two hundred and fifty yards. In Ajaccio and Bastia they can be even more costly.

If, however, as may well be the case, you are forced to call a cab, pick one of the more ramshackle-looking types. Not only are these cheaper, but they are usually provided with meters. In the resorts, such as Calvi, Propriano, and Ajaccio, the taxi business appears to be in the casual hands of some hard cases who thrive over the wheels of glossy Buicks and Studeys, and whose prices are proportionately princely. What's more, one can't haggle with these youths, many of whom are tough Marseillais. But get them to state a price first; this may seem an unpleasant necessity to us diffident English, but don't forget that for these types it's normal. Entirely what they expect. You can treat the whole thing in a completely relaxed manner, therefore.

Don't tip these non-metered youths, unless of course one of them performs a special service for you. Such, in my opinion, is not too likely with these pseudo-American operators. However, the veteran metered drivers should be given a percentage of their charge.

## ELECTRICITY

Well laid on throughout the island. In Ajaccio and Bastia functioning one hundred per cent. You will also be surprised, if you shave electrically, at the out-of-the-way places, including camping sites, which carry outlets for electric razors. This should not encourage you to take electric gadgets, however. Will your plug-ends fit the French sockets? Will you blow your brand-new Remington shaver to smithereens on unconverted current? (34)

Some of the smaller towns, like Cargèse for example, have an erratic service. Do not take anything therefore,

---

(34) Generally 110-115 volts A.C.; travelling irons should be equipped with 3-way plugs to enable them to work in 110, 160, or 220 sockets.

as I did, on which you want to rely (such as a portable electric typewriter). Do take a couple of candles, packed in a plastic sponge-bag (they melt), some sturdy English matches (French matches wilt), an efficient lighter, or a torch. The last is a must, if motoring.

## SICKNESS

In case of any emergency the principal hospital in Ajaccio is the Hospice Civil Ste.-Eugénie. Private clinics include: the Clinique Chirurgicale Ajaccienne (Dr. Guglielmi), the Clinique Menasse (Dr. Alfred Menasse) on the Cours Grandval, and the Clinique Comiti (Dr. Paul Comiti) on the Boulevard Albert-Premier. The following doctor is highly recommended to me: Dr. J. L. Luciani, 6 Rue Emmanuel Arène, Ajaccio.

# PART TWO

ROUND THE COAST

In drawing up this survey of the Corsican coastline, it seemed tidiest and most logical to start off in the capital of the island, Ajaccio, and then circulate clockwise. Secondly, after some consideration, it also seemed more helpful to give distances in kilometres rather than in miles. There are pros and cons involved in this decision, I know, but every sign you see on the island will be marked in kms. The white distance stones at the sides of the roads, as well as the milometer of your car if you hire it there. In short, one soon comes to "think in" kilometres in Corsica, as on the continent generally. My system will merely be mildly inconveniencing to those who take their own British cars with them, with milometers in miles. Actually, these can be adjusted to kilometres before setting out, if you wish, and in any case an easy conversion table can be found at the back of this book. The principle of converting kilometres to miles can be stated as follows: *Multiply by five and divide by eight.*

My scheme can be used in any way, of course. Should you land at Bastia with your car, you can begin there and continue clockwise with me or, if you prefer to go in the reverse direction, you can look up Bastia in the pages that follow and work backwards. For my plan is going to be to cover the intermediary routes between towns relatively briefly, italicizing places of interest, and then stop in detail at each town of importance, where you are likely to want to stay. Incidentally, although it's risky to generalize too far on this point, the trend of

French tourist traffic in the season tends to be from Bastia towards Ajaccio, either through the island or round the coast. Travelling in my direction, you will have the advantage of meeting this traffic, rather than getting stuck behind it en route.

In any case, whatever you choose to do, *bon voyage*!

## AJACCIO

*Hotels:*

des Etrangers (tel.: 1-26)
Grand Hôtel Continental (tel.: 0-16)
Impérial (tel.: 0-62)

Also: Bella Vista — Belvédère — Colomba — De la Poste — Des Liserons — Les Mouettes — Peytavy — Solemare — others are being constructed as I write.

My recommendations: Hôtel des Etrangers. This is a charming hotel with forty rooms, set slightly back from the busy Cours Grandval, in the leafy little Rue Rossi, and thus accordingly quiet. It has a garden, a delightful bar with a nautical flavour, and a fine cuisine; all in all, the atmosphere is most congenial and the management friendly. It is, however, necessary to take two meals a day here (any two). The Grand Hôtel, close by, is twice as large and very different in feeling, an ugly but comfortable building. The Impérial is right on the sea front, along the Boulevard Albert-Premier, which can be noisy at night in the seasonal months. I recommend it less unreservedly. All these hotels have good views over the gulf.

If you want to be more modest, save your money, and also feel free to take all your meals out in the town, I recommend one of the several excellent hotels without restaurants, such as the Colomba, De la Poste, Les

124

Mouettes, or Solemare. (35) These are usually converted houses, with little or no lounge facilities, but with breakfast, laundry, and other services available, should you wish. They are run in a more casual, perhaps even slightly haphazard manner, which can often contribute to one's sense of relaxation on holiday. I particularly liked the Solemare, two lovely old villas knocked together on the sea front in the Boulevard Lantivy; its rooms are light, airy, and have been tastefully furnished in a generally modern manner. Family pensions include the very moderately priced Pension des Liserons, 50 Cours Napoléon, whose rates are most reasonable and whose proprietor, M. Blanck-Poli, will make you most comfortable. The best camping establishment is five kilometres out along the Route des Sanguinaires, called Santa Lina.

Outside Ajaccio there are two more hotels worth recommending: just before you reach the Santa Lina there is the Hôtel de la Corniche. In the other direction there is a perfectly delightful little hotel called Le Maquis at Porticcio, overlooking the sea fifteen kilometres southeast of the town across the bay. This only has eleven rooms and it is essential to reserve in advance since it is much used by week-ending Ajacciens. But it is worth a visit, if you have a car and don't mind a roughish road.

*Restaurants:*

Côte d'Azur
Les Gourmets
Du Plat d'Or
U Fuconu
De France.

My recommendations: Ajaccio is replete with restaurants, the majority of which are of a similar standard. Anyway

(35) Not to be confused with a well-known *camping*, some thirty kilometres out of the town, called Mare e Sole.

half the fun of exploring a new town is making one's own " finds." Do not miss, however, having a sumptuous meal at the Côte d'Azur, two rough-plastered rooms over the main Cours Napoléon (and, by the way, never let the modesty of a setting put you off a restaurant in Corsica, it's no guide one way or the other to the standard of cooking on hand). You have to walk up a flight of stone steps to the Côte d'Azur, but the menu can always be inspected at street level. The food here is superb, there is a Swiss chef, and the service is most hospitable: try one of their steaks *au beurre d'anchois*. A colossal slice of tender meat will arrive mounted on a crouton and dripping with anchovy butter. A little further along the Cours Napoléon, on the other side, is the excellent Les Gourmets. Neither of these restaurants serves *al fresco* and it must even be confessed that the setting of Les Gourmets is comparatively dreary. Since the English like to eat out on holiday I recommend a stroll in and around the Place Foch where there are several pleasant outdoor restaurants, with views over the quayside. These are much of a muchness with regard to the food. U Fuconu, in the Rue Général Campi, boasts a repertoire of Corsican delicacies, and the Du Plat d'Or, near the Post Office, a garden.

*Museums:*

> Maison Bonaparte
> Musée Napoléonien
> Musée and Palais Fesch
> Chapelle Impériale.

You can see (or "do") all these in a morning. Napoleon's birth-place is in a side-street off the Rue Bonaparte and the bedroom where he was born has been made into a little shrine really, emphasizing, with its simple furnishing, worn parquet, and the old sofa where his mother gave sudden birth, the very humble beginnings of this great man. There is a definite atmosphere here as there is, of another sort, in the Musée Napoléonien. This Museum is to be found, within two minutes' walk, inside the Hôtel de Ville or Town Hall in the Place Foch, where are also the offices of the *Syndicat d'Initiative Régional d'Ajaccio et de la Corse,* "Essitac" as it is called, presided over by a friend to his country if ever there was one. The Musée Napoléonien is quartered in the Grand Salon on the first floor of this building (concierge on this floor, tip her); the room is worth a visit if you want to sense, almost tangibly, the atmosphere of the Empire. There are paintings of the Bonaparte family by Gérard, Winterhalter, and Girodet; there is also a Canova sculpture of the Cardinal Fesch, Primate of Lyon, Napoleon's uncle and celebrated benefactor of Ajaccio. But with its dark paper, its huge chandelier pressing overhead, this room leaves an enormously theatrical impression, as if one were wandering through some Cecil Beaton setting. The Musée and Palais Fesch are another two minutes away, down the narrow Rue Fesch. There is another statue of the Cardinal here and, as you face the Palace, the left wing houses the library and museum, the right the Imperial Chapel where several members of the Bonaparte family, its chief member excepted, lie buried. And there are further family portraits here. The Fesch Museum is a modest attempt within a very limited gallery to represent, chiefly for the use of local students, the various principal schools of painting. The pictures on display are occasionally loaned from the Louvre and other collections for this admirable purpose, and one cannot always be exact as to what is being shown; but when I last went there, some fine primitives were on display, also a Botticelli *Virgin* and a

127

Titian *Leda*. Outside Ajaccio there are two places of interest in this category which I should mention: two kilometres in the direction of the Iles Sanguinaires there is the early seventeenth-century Chapelle des Grecs, while some thirteen kilometres north-west (take road D 61 to Matoni) can be seen the Château de la Punta, an elegant reproduction of one of the burnt Tuileries pavilions (of the stones of which it was in fact built), paintings by Gérard and Boucher, and magnificent views to either side. I need hardly add that Ajaccio is stiff with statues to Napoleon, a name not to be taken lightly there. He stands, mounted, as a Roman Emperor with a globe of the world in one one hand, staring southwards over the bay from the Place Charles-de-Gaulle (a statue "after" Viollet-le-Duc): and you will run into him, too, in the costume of his times at the end of the heavily shaded Boulevard Général-Leclerc which continues the Cours Grandval. Near this latter monument may be seen Napoleon's grotto where legend once had it that he used to like to go and meditate; however, the more austere scholarship of modern times has disallowed this possibility.

*Night-life*: Limited. You can dance at the Casino which fronts the sea just below the Place Charles-de-Gaulle, but it is not an especially attractive place. At both this Casino, and that at Ile Rousse, you can gamble cheaply at *boule*, a kind of roulette. Out on the Route des Sanguinaires there are three *"cafés-dancings,"* as the French call them —Palm-Beach, Marinella, and Neptune. These are right over the sea and rather more fun. It should be said that Corsica is not, perhaps fortunately, organized for " niteries." Nor is there, it seems, much if any prostitution: no " sea-gulls," as they say. Other diversions in the capital now include one theatre and two cinemas.

128

6.         Erbalunga: looking south down the coast of Cap Corse; Bastia can
                     be seen in the distance.

7.         Bastia: the Citadelle, dominating the entrance to the New Port.

18. Bastia : a typical street scene in the Old Town.

19. Bastia harbour.

*Post Office:* Large building in the middle of the Cours Napoléon. You can't miss it!

*Banks:* See under "Currency" information in Part I.

*Beaches:* The best ones, with the finest sand, are to be found along the Route des Sanguinaires. In the summer a bus service (plainly marked SERVICE DES PLAGES) runs every half-hour to these little coves, which have such names as (in their order) Scudo and Ariadne. But don't worry about these, simply take a bus out until you see a spot of sand that seems inviting enough, and get out and stroll. If you want to go on farther than the PLAGES bus, then take the bus marked TOUR DE LA PARATA. In fact, if you are fairly broke and can't afford to move around Corsica, you can still have a very good holiday in Ajaccio itself, taking the bus out to these plages every day. Many French students do this and you can see them toasting themselves all along the coast here. This Route des Sanguinaires (sometimes nicknamed the Appian Way owing to the colossal cemeteries that bound it on one side) is attractive, the sea a glorious green, and the sand like shot silk. In the other direction out of Ajaccio, towards Porticcio, you come to the huge, curving Ricardo plage, behind which (though out of sight when you are bathing) lies the airport. The sand here is again excellent, but the sea shelves more steeply. Thanks to its vast length it is never crowded. Take your choice. No instructions are necessary if you are motoring to the West out of Ajaccio; you simply take the only road available. To reach Ricardo beach, however, which now has its own restaurant set-up too, you drive East out of the town, keeping to N 196 (36) and ignoring the turn-off to Corte to your left. About three kilometres from the latter you climb a hill and find a

(36) The N used in these French markings is really an abbreviation of *Route Nationale,* i.e., major road.

E

bridge. Turn right here over the bridge for both airport and plage. Do *not* think, however, that by simply keeping on going you will reach those tempting fans of sand you see on the very far side of the bay! These are clustered around Porticcio and, at present, you can only get through to them by continuing on N 196 and turning right just before Pisciatello. However, new roads are being made along here and the conditions of the present ones are constantly being improved. The facilities at the beaches also develop annually; there is now water-skiing to be had, quite cheaply, at two of these places.

*Excursions:* By sea—there are numerous tours that can be made by motor-boat, or *vedette*. Simply walk down the Place Foch to the Quai Napoléon and look for the sign PROMENADE EN MER (which does not mean that you will walk on water). These boats take you round the gulf to the Iles Sanguinaires and usually leave at nine and three.

By road—there are all sorts and manners of bus excursions, if you have not laid anything on beforehand. Try inquiring at the office of Corse-tourisme, 5 Place Foch. *British Consulate:* 13 Boulevard Albert-Premier (tel.: 6-65).

*Essitac:* Syndicat d'Initiative Régional d'Ajaccio et de la Corse, Hôtel de Ville, Place du Maréchal-Foch (tel.: 2-87). See also under Bastia. In Paris, consult: Jean Ollandini et l'Office de Tourisme Corse, 9 Rue de l'Echelle.

Ajaccio, "the white city" as it has been called, is really the Corsican Naples. With its hill background, its bluish gulf sweeping round to your left, and the islands called Bloody falling away to your right, it is a gentler and more beautiful setting than Naples—an opinion which, by the way, you need not be ashamed to share, since it was that of Edward VII. Ajaccio has a most summery air even in winter and, with its villas and palms, its richly leafy squares, it extends an inviting hand to the visitor. Deriving its name from Ajax (or, according to another tradition, from Cyrnos' son, Aiazzo), it numbers between thirty and thirty-five thousand inhabitants, most of whom seem to parade down the colourful Cours Napoléon, the main artery of the town, and pour into the Place Charles-de-Gaulle each evening.

This evening parade, enlivened as it is by touchingly beautiful girls sauntering arm-in-arm, chatting and giggling, is of course a feature of Mediterranean life—the *passegiata* —and should not be missed. It is not by the local swains, believe me!

The city, a prefecture and bishopric, is built in a hemi-cycle bordered by hills of olive and orange-trees and I can't think of any place of its size where one is made so happily conscious of the sea at all times. Alphonse Daudet, who adored Ajaccio, felt strongly aware of this and wrote of "the view to the horizon, so lovely in the way that, in the spaces between the leaves, the sea painted blue patterns which scintillated like pieces of broken glass and danced in the shimmering air. There was the distant sound of the sea, a cadenced murmur that cradled one like some invisible ship."

Now for a few final suggestions. To get a true feel of this gulf of pleasure you should early in your stay walk or drive up the hill behind the city toward the Peraldi Chapel. Follow the Cours Grandval until you come to Napoleon's statue and then turn right. On your way you can see the pathway known as the Promenade des Anglais and rest on a bench amid yucca and aloe, and you can also visit the Salario Fountain, whose name is taken from

131

the salamanders originally abounding there, and then walk along the so-called Crest Road (Chemin des Crêtes). You will find these paths much frequented in the evenings for the view over Ajaccio is so sharp it is as if one is seeing the capital from a plane, while the panorama of hill and gulf extending on either hand is incomparable. There is, incidentally, an excellent hotel up here called the Highland (tel.: 5-17), one of the most expensive in Ajaccio. This is quite a fair walk from the town, four or five kilometres up a steep hill, but elsewhere in Ajaccio everything is well within easy walking distance. In both Ajaccio and Bastia, the two largest towns on the island, you can reach everything on foot without any trouble at all and, as a matter of fact, there was one period in Ajaccio when I used to leave my car at my hotel most of the time thanks, principally, to some new and officious arrivals among the local gendarmes, a brace of bobbies keen as mustard who seemed to delight in ticking off and faulting foreign drivers. (37)

Secondly, you will always in Corsica be attracted into strolling around the Old Town (or *vieille ville*) of any new place you are visiting; in common with most other ports on the island, Ajaccio is so to speak hinged on its Citadel. You can walk along the quayside to the Jetée de la Citadelle right under this, but the fortress itself is in use and

---

(37) I ought to add that this was exceptional. Outside Calvi and Ajaccio I've usually found Corsican police fairly lenient and courteous. But they can be tough and, despite those deceptively graceful balletic motions they go through on their pedestals when directing traffic, they sometimes show their teeth to fast-driving French in no uncertain manner. In Ajaccio there are (almost invisible) yellow pedestrian crossing lines to watch for and *don't* park between the No Parking signs on the Quai Napoléon. These are reserved for V.I.P.'s and it makes the police *awfully cross* if you do. Most towns in Corsica observe alternate-day parking on either side of the street.

there are certain hours of the day when you are not allowed to drive round there. These hours may be seen listed on a noticeboard just in front of it in a street named after a local victim of Auschwitz, Danièle Casanova. The streets in this part are Neapolitanly narrow and you will easily come across the Cathedral here, with its rather lovely cupola. Notice also, facing west from the Citadel, one of the most elegant villas in Ajaccio. Flanked with fine palm trees, this is appropriately the residence of the present incumbent of one of the oldest names in Corsica.

Thirdly, and I have left this to last for emphasis, you should see the Iles Sanguinaires. These are a group of conical islands that straggle out from the Pointe de la Parata (under the eye of a characteristic Genoese tower of this name), some twelve kilometres west of the town— actually a little bit more than this by my register. In the evening they turn multi-coloured in the rays of the setting sun and are rather beautiful; if one came upon this spot unexpectedly one would doubtless be enchanted. But unfortunately the Iles Sanguinaires have been over publicized and it is hard to see them now with anything approaching a pristine eye. As a matter of fact, on a grey day they looked rather dull. The largest and most distant of the group — the Grande Sanguinaire or Mezzo Mare, as it is called — was also visited by Daudet in the eighteen sixties, when he was secretary to the Duc de Morny; it has a lighthouse run by a few officials who are today the only inhabitants of the islands. There is a convenient restaurant at the Pointe de la Parata where you can watch the sunset, the *coucher du soleil*, but the general atmosphere is too reminiscent of Beachy Head to be attractive to me.

# FROM AJACCIO TO CARGÈSE
## (51½ kilometres)

A glorious drive to start off with, but only one of many of its kind. Leave Ajaccio down the Cours Napoléon as if making for the airport; or, if you wish to avoid the traffic in this busy thoroughfare, follow the quays and come up into the Cours where it turns into the Boulevard Jean Nicoli. Corsican towns are quite simple and you cannot really lose your way. The turn-off to your left is well marked at a large petrol station — you take the Corte road, N 193. Actually, there are two big petrol garages at present along this road out but the one at the turn-off is right astride the fork. Use it to fill 'er up, if necessary, and check oil and tyre pressures because the next good repairs garage is 163 kilometres away, at Calvi.

You then follow N 193, a fast road, for seven kilometres until you come to Mezzavia, with more petrol pumps on your left as you approach. Here you turn left on N 199 clearly marked for Calvi. You drive under the stone aqueduct which serves Ajaccio with water and start climbing a goodish road to the Col de Listincone, with fine views of the gulf falling back behind you. After this pass you descend briefly and then start the twisty climb up to the *Col de San-Bastiano* (437 metres), named after a little chapel to Saint Sebastian just off the road. It is worth stopping here because as you mount the final rise and see the signboard marking the place on your left a breath-taking view of the Gulf of Sagone spreads out in front of you; at the same time, to your left, to the south-west, that is, a valley thick with *maquis* drops off to the Gulf of Lava, where incidentally one of the last great bandits, Romanetti, was killed in 1926. (38) But the *Golfe de Sagone*

(38) For a good French bandit book, including a section on Nonce Romanetti, see: Pierre Bonardi, *Les Rois du Maquis,* Paris; André Delpeuch, 1926.

is superb, stretch after stretch of sand visible against the backdrop of mountain and sea. You then wind down from the Col. In doing so, do not take the turn-off slightly to the right marked for Sari-d'Orcino, unless you want to see a verdant little village with nice white houses called *Calcatoggio* on your way. I stress this because the Sari-d'Orcino road is good and appears at first to lead straight ahead. No, bear to your left and keep dipping to the bay.

In doing so you will cross the Liscia, a small stream which runs into a bay of the same name; you can turn off a minor track to the left here and take a bathe on a vast stretch of sand on which I have scarcely ever seen a soul. But in stormy weather the waves on this beach can be what the West Indians of the Caribbean call "dumpers" —I speak from experience!

Continuing, you will leave to your right the ruins of the thirteenth-century *Castle of Capraja,* once the residence of the Cinarca Counts (see the reference to Giudice in my section on "History" above). You then circle another Genoese tower, this one called Capigliolo, and hit another perfect beach, cosier than the Tiuccia-Liscia beach, which has a rather arid immediate background. But if you like sand, it can truly be said that there are nothing but perfect beaches all the way along to Cargèse and beyond it. Few of these have been exploited much, either. Such is to come, I fear. After this beach, you cross another stream, the Liamone, in an avenue of splendid eucalyptus and soon find two more beaches around Sagone.

A bishopric in the sixth century, Sagone was utterly razed by Barbary corsairs — the wall belonging to its old cathedral may still be seen. There are a couple of simple hotels here, one overlooking a nearby beach; of the two I recommend the Cyrnos. The village itself is no more really than a collection of fishermen's houses. However, I ran across a young French couple quartered very happily en pension here. Sagone is 38 kilometres from Ajaccio. Cargèse lies another 13½ on.

Bear to your left out of Sagone, another pleasantly leafy avenue, and then start an easy climb into Cargèse itself. Two or three kilometres before you come into the town, there is a *camping* to the left by the sea which is one of those I can heartily recommend, if you want to sample this kind of life. This is called the Camp du Carré d'As or *Rocca-Marina* and you will find its entrance at the top of a slope nearing Cargèse. Entering, prepare to plunge down a fiendish track to a lovely little bay with perfect sand fringed with emerald shrubs. Here you will find clean bungalows and good cooking (better than in either of the Cargèse hotels, I might say). The proprietor and his wife, the Perriers, are the most hospitable couple imaginable and there is a delightfully friendly atmosphere about. In the summer, however, like all such places, it gets extremely crowded, but the place is run with discrimination and I assure you that waking up in the morning in this little bay you savour that country silence, and sense of infinite peace, which make Corsica so attractive today.

## CARGESE

*Hotels:*

Cyrnos (tel.: 3).
Thalassa.

My recommendations: Cyrnos is in the town; the Thalassa is right on the best plage. Both are small, with clean rooms but mediocre cooking. The Thalassa, run by a friendly young man, is obviously more attractive for prospective bathers.

*Petrol Pump:* run by the restaurant on the main road.

Cargèse is a not uninteresting village with a good deal of its own character still intact. It was founded in 1676 by Peloponnese Greeks evading Turkish tyranny and still possesses a Greek Catholic, as well as a Roman Catholic, church. Outside the former, by the way, is a grand example of a tree you will occasionaly spot in Corsica, the *belombra,* a gnarled tree about the size of a very large olive which gives the impression of suffering from elephantiasis of the roots.

Cargèse is, then, the only Greek village in the island. Constructed in amphitheatre form on a block of granite which falls sheer down to a little port, its streets might have been drawn on a ruler and are very different in feeling from the usual winding Corsican streets. As it happens, too, Greek is still taught in the school at Cargèse. If you are interested in finding out more about the Greek settlements here, there is a delightful section on Cargèse in Patrick Leigh Fermor's *Mani.*

Since the town is so close to Ajaccio it is neglected by tourists, who mostly drive straight on to Piana and Calvi, thus missing the fine beach just north of the town. This is a few hundred yards down a good track which branches to the left off the main Piana road out. The sand here is again good and one can keep well to oneself.

## FROM CARGESE TO PIANA
### (19½ kilometres)

You leave Cargèse, holding to the right as the road winds out of the town, still on N 199 which takes you all the way along the coast to Cap Corse. You drop down and start making inland for your next objective, Piana.

If you are a bather keen on finding isolated beaches, however, let me urge you to try a dip in the magnificent

*Golfe de Chioni* (39) which you will see clearly to your left, as you descend. Very few tourists (or even locals) know how to get to it, the only foreigners I know who have been there have gone by boat; so, believe me, this information is well worth the price of admission!

The best way I can direct you is as follows: two bridges carry two streams, the Lomberlaccio and Fornello, into one current, the Chioni, which pours into the far, northern end of the bay. (There is actually a third bridge, but it is over a dry gulch). *Before* you reach these little bridges, travelling in this direction, there is a small branch track to the left, an evil-looking goat path you may not want to take your car down. But it is quite safe to do so. The beginning part is the worst, or was when I was last there. Alternatively you can park off the road near a small fountain and walk — a few hundred yards. Simply follow this track and make for the beach; you will have to cross fields and push through hedges, but it is worth it. The beach is absolutely marvellous, there is never anyone there, and you can do exactly what you like. If you want to be more adventurous still, you can walk to the top end of the bay, where the Chioni comes in, cross the hill by the Genoese tower, and you will find another heavenly beach, much smaller, right beneath you.

The initial track off the main road is, I admit, reasonably easy to miss, since it is at first heavily overhung by trees. Let me add this. Just before you reach the final bridge I have mentioned above there is, at the left of the road as you start the climb up to Piana, a plaque commemorating the landing of the submarine *Casabianca* during the last war to make contact with Corsican partisans. If you pass this, then you have gone about two kilometres too far,

---

(39) As already noted, the locals pronounce *o* like our *u*: thus— Ky-*ooo*-ny.

I'd say. Coming from the Piana side, of course, this stone memorial acts as a good reminder that you are close to the turn-off.

The climb up to Piana is, as I have already noted, a sickening one. Hillsides which, to all accounts, were once lushly verdant are today blackened and deserted. Not a bird about. All in all, a grim warning against forest fires. Watch your children.

Once you have climbed the hill the road levels out and you come to a couple of little Cols from which your first sight of the finest red rock country in the world may be obtained. You swing into Piana rather suddenly and should be warned to hug the right, rather than driving down to the old church, round which will undoubtedly be seated a noble selection of those elderly Corsican gentlemen, with thick moustaches, scarlet cummerbunds, pipes, and velveteen jackets, watching you as they have, in their lives, watched so many others enter Piana.

## PIANA

*Hotels:*

> Des Roches Rouges (tel.: 1)
> Continental (tel: 2)
> Des Calanches (tel.: 8).

My recommendations: All three are satisfactory, but I must confess that in this case I am prejudiced since the Hôtel des Roches Rouges happens to be one of my favourite places on earth. From the majority of its 56 rooms you will be able to enjoy one of the finest views it is possible to see—and I speak as a fair traveller. In fact, the view over the gulfs of Porto and Girolata which extend before you in fold after fold of mountain scenery is practically a Corsican institution by now, but this time you need have no fear of anything being over-written. Stroll out on to the terrace your first evening and you will notice how the whole world seems to become more visible and audible from this elevation. An immense solemnity of nature pervades the place and there are times, as a sombre sun is sinking, when it seems a sacrilege to speak on that terrace! As a matter of fact, I have always noticed how subdued people's voices become there. The sunsets here can be seen, by some trick of optical angles, with astonishing precision, far more clearly than at Porto, and a few evenings watching them, as the distant villages start to burn like diamonds on their iron-coloured hills, will soon dissolve your cares. These sunsets merit some good photography, too. Apart from all this, the Roches Rouges is splendidly run by M. Pandolfi, a gentleman hotelier who knows his onions, I assure you. The food is first-rate, the service charming, and there is plenty of good garage space. This ugly, rambling old house with its fowls and donkeys on the patient prowl, its outhouses full of old doors, mattresses, discarded boilers, and big chests, has a gloriously peaceful air about it, and you owe it to yourself to give it a few days at the very least, for Piana to work its spell upon you. The bedrooms are in some cases delightfully papered, there are brass-knobbed bedsteads, and little wooden balconies. The hotel lacks bars, dancing, radios, and so forth and because of this, and because there is no plage on its doorstep, it has been given the go-by by the average French and foreign tourist. May this state of affairs long continue, so far as I'm concerned! Finally, as an instance of just how misleading "official" information can be, let me point out that the Roches Rouges is marked as ***C in the French Government Year-Book of Corsican hotels. If you check this listing against the category of

140

"Features" provided, you will find the words, "Not so well situated"!!

*Restaurants:* There are a few bars (no *essence*), one of which is called the Cave des Corsaires and is worth a visit for the excellent guitarist on hand. Also, some good muscat if you like it. This tiny bar, situated just behind the church, is quite easy to find. For all I know the guitarist may be phony, i.e. he may be French not Corsican at all; I don't know and frankly I don't care too much, since he did play extraordinarily well.

Piana town is not a pretty place at all, but it has the merit of being authentic. To tell the truth, the inhabitants are rapidly making it even uglier by tossing out their rubbish down an open hillside, visible from the Roches Rouges. (40) Still, it does have that genuine quality one finds in fishing villages with a life of their own, and the church tower, with its worn enamel face, is most attractive. In front of the Post Office there is also a pleasant fountain presented by Napoleon III.

A road is being laboriously driven down to the little Marine de Ficajola, which the Pianese refer to as their plage, a beautiful creek seemingly miles and miles below the town. From local conversations I gathered that this road, privately financed, will still take some time to complete (it has already taken three years). But if you are fit, or aren't and ought to be, I thoroughly

---

(40) I refuse to sentimentalize. At Piana, confronted with the very finest natural scenery imaginable, I found the local population nightly glued to the "goggle-box," watching with glee old Harold Lloyd and Chaplin shorts beamed, very badly, from Marseille. David Dodge, writing in a recent issue of *Holiday* magazine, seems to corroborate my opinion: " Young Corsica doesn't fight vendettas. . . . It snaps its fingers in front of the island's rare jukeboxes, or stares hungrily at a few poor television images dimly received from the mainland. . . ."

recommend a day on the Ficajola plage; it will take you a 45 minutes' walk down and a hard climb back of anything up to an hour—I did it back to the church in 48 minutes flat once and didn't feel the same until I'd had eight glasses of lager. Get the waiter or waitress at the Roches Rouges to direct you *carefully;* you start off on a path leading down from a little gate in the garden and continue downwards—*sempre girando*—until you strike a small stream. The country is lovely. On one side rise the first of the red rock calanches and on the other thick verdure, chirruping with birds and plashy with cascades. Finally, you come out past some fishermen's huts into the peerless bay itself, where the sea is a transparent turquoise. All along the coast here the land slopes abruptly and you will soon find yourself staring straight down from the surface of the sea at fish 30 or more feet below you (the Gulf of Porto sinks to 400 metres within a very short distance). The bathing at Ficajola is perfectly safe, as it is not near Porto; and don't imagine that there are too many fishermen about when you first get down there—they will disappear as the sun also rises. For most of these chaps work fantastically hard in the summers and, since they get up around three in the morning, they sleep nearly all afternoon. Take the trip back easily, though. The toughest part comes near the end. And when you get back to Piana, try some of the incomparable water from a local spring, or *source,* it's really much better than the beer!

## FROM PIANA TO PORTO
### (11 kilometres)

This stretch of road, almost all downhill, takes you *en corniche* through that lunar landscape known as *Les Calanches,* or Calanques. These comprise one of the natural wonders of Corsica and well live up to their international reputation. They are huge formations of red rock, rising sheer from the sea in great tormented peaks, like so many petrified avalanches, honeycombed with holes. Against their skull-like formations the green of the forests stands out with tremendous vividness. There is a restaurant, the Chalet des Roches Rouges, on the way here and I advise a stop. The proprietor is understandably proud of his fine site in the middle of all this torrentially slashed granite, and he will show you rock formations which invite you to imagine living shapes, stone topiary work, as it were—a monk confessing a penitent, a bear, a tortoise, an eagle, odd stones balanced on top of each other. Frankly, this sort of game means little to me but the rock scenery is superb. I have never seen anything like it anywhere else. Again, *please don't leave litter*. The last time I sat in this restaurant, imbibing a cool Tuborg, the view was ruined for me by the fact that a group of English were slowly and steadily tossing orange-peel into it.

The road spirals hectically into Porto and I counsel extreme caution, if driving. The corners are precipitous and infrequently walled in. One has to use one's horn pretty continually. If you are a camper, you should drop off to the left before reaching the bridge into Porto itself. This will take you down into an heroic eucalyptus grove where the Porto river trickles placidly into the gulf. This is one of the loveliest camping sites imaginable. And let me lastly add that you can walk fairly comfortably from Piana to Porto, but not back; if walking, you do not follow the roads, but rather a small path indicated by painted marks (pale blue when I last saw them) which cut down across the twists of road.

# PORTO

*Hotels:*

Bella Vista (tel.: Ota 8)
Le Colombo (tel.: Porto 14).

*My recommendations:* Both are good, about the same size and rank. I perhaps prefer the Colombo, whose patron, M. Milleli, is actively engaged in promoting the tourist trade and is in fact, a local Syndicat d'Initiative President. These hotels are in the leafy section of Porto known as Bellavista and, as you approach from Piana, beyond the bridge and up the hill to the right on the Calvi road. If you take the left fork after the bridge, you will be led down to the Marine where, around a small jetty, there is a cluster of new hotels and restaurants. I found this unattractively touristy but there are at least four hotels there which looked satisfactory, I haven't personally stayed in any of them, I'm afraid.

*Restaurants:* try Du Soleil Couchant (also an hotel) on the Marine.

*Petrol pump:* run by the restaurant near the bridge.

Porto is situated around the estuary of the river of that name as it debouches into the gulf. With the magnificent Spelunca gorge lowering behind it, the village is in a fine natural setting. It is, however, one of the most photographed resorts in Corsica and there is a feeling of organization here which I confess not to my taste. The hoteliers and restaurateurs, here more than anywhere on the island, except possibly Propriano, seem keen to clip another Croesus from beyond the seas. The estuary itself is a deep shingle beach, heavy stones having been driven up by high seas in the past few years; it makes quite an unappealing desert to cross from the camping area, I felt. But the trees are lovely and the bay offers goodish bathing up to a point. Up to, in fact, *the* point, which you will see mounted with another Genoese watch-tower. Beyond this it is said not to be safe to venture. Odd currents operating beyond this promontory have pulled the best swimmers down. They fished a French girl out, after two days' immersion, when I was there once. And one sees the odd drowned dog drifting in, swollen and bruised-looking from a battering on the rocks. Unpleasant warnings. It was here, around the reef called La Secca, that the film *The Two Companions* was made.

But don't let me run Porto down unduly. One can stay there and bathe quite safely, so long as one is prudent. Dozens do, every year. And the views in the evening are sheer Day-glo, believe me, just flamboyantly grandiose.

## FROM PORTO TO CALVI
### (81 kilometres)

As already remarked above, I have heard this called the most beautiful road in the world by an experienced motorist. You climb abruptly out of Porto and from now on, in fact, should resign yourself to not using top gear for quite a while. A few kilometres out you will see to your left an excellent little plage at *Bussaglia;* this can be reached relatively comfortably by branch track, but there are other, temptingly white inlets here that you can only come at by mule-track or boat. Don't attempt—yet—to reach them in your car.

Wonderful views of the Gulf of Porto, deep blue against the rosy Calanches, assail you as you swing up through the curved village of *Partinello* and attain the summit of the *Col de la Croix*. You will almost undoubtedly be tempted (especially if you are a keen photographer) to stop to admire the view either here or at the slightly higher *Col de*

145

*Palmarella,* about ten kilometres further on. Pines and oak behind you and deep beneath, in its infinite azure, the *Gulf of Girolata.* The nap of the sea seems dark as a bird's wing here. The entire coastline is really superb. The map (Michelin) marks forests to either side but for much of the way this is merely high *maquis,* rather than trees. The ravines thicken and the water in the pebbly streams strewn about the mountains seems clearer and clearer.

You then descend and the road improves. Whitish rocks here. Then there is a good straight stretch (where I blew out doing ninety) beside the Fango river — which you turn right to cross, over a biggish, ugly bridge, leaving the road to Galeria to continue ahead. The map makes it look as if you had only come about a third of your way, but you are actually, owing to the constant twists up to the Palmarella pass, well over half-way to Calvi here.

There is more enticing coastal scenery now, as you pass on your right the ruined silver mine of *Argentella.* Coming into Calvi itself, a peninsula runs out to your left to the point of *Revellata,* where a powerful lighthouse has been mounted on red rocks and where the famous Seal Cave, or *Grotte des Veaux Marins,* may be visited.


## CALVI

*Hotels:*

    Calvi Palace (tel.: 32)
    Kallisté (tel.: 2)
    Grand Hotel (tel.: 5)
    Nord-Sud.

My recommendations: The Palace is my choice. As it is, I might add, of a considerable number of English people in the summer. It is run with great gusto by a thoroughly professional hotelier, M. Biasini, and has one of the best all-round cuisines in Corsica. Even in the most crowded moments, both bedroom and dining service (much of which is French) are impeccable, and the hotel closely overlooks the beach. I strongly recommend it. But it is an hotel that needs a reservation in advance.

Both the Grand (which changes traveller's cheques, by the way) and Palace are fairly close to each other on the road out to Ile Rousse, and so command magnificent views to the mountains across the bay. The North-Sud, also satisfactory, is on the other side of the town and I am afraid I, for one, have had too much of Army life to appreciate its proximity to the Citadel. The Kallisté is too much in the town, which can be a noisy one at night in the season. Indeed, that Calvi is a highly frequented resort is well attested by the fact that the Palace has sixty rooms and the Grand fifty. All of these hotels are simple by sophisticated standards and none has adequate lounge space; but the Palace is remarkably well-run.

*Restaurants:*
    Chez François
    Aux Bons Amis
    Ile-de-Beauté.

My recommendations: There is a line of restaurants of similar quality along the quayside. All have menus up outside. I merely list some I have eaten at, and which were good, especially the first-named, just off the port. I might also mention here that there are more semi-expensive boutiques at Calvi than in Ajaccio or Bastia, where the shops are mainly straight commercial stores.

*Night-life:*
    Chez Tao
    Au Son des Guitares
    Les Palmiers.

There are others. As possibly the most sophisticated resort on the island, Calvi is one place that has dancing thoroughly laid on. If you like the Palais de Danse atmosphere, Les Palmiers right on the port will provide it. A band blares there every night. To this music you can jive gently or jumpily, as you desire, and there's usually a "crooner" or two on hand to make the accompaniment look fairly defenseless. Should you prefer a less continuous cannonade, however, and an "intimate" atmosphere, I recommend Au Son des Guitares. It generally features Corsican guitarists and is widely known. Then there is Chez Tao. Yes, indeed. This night-club is run in three or four rooms of the old Guibega Palace in the Citadel; it is surely appropriate that this fifteenth-century home of the erstwhile Bishops of Sagone should now be in the capable hands of a White Russian emigré and former Cossack dancer, Count Tao Kerekoff, who conducts affairs with considerable *brio*. I don't know if he still does this, but there was a time when it was Tao's custom to call the customers to order at midnight to sing the Coriscan national anthem, *L'Ajacienne*. After this gesture — *plus Corse que les Corses*, as it were — the lights were doused and one was sternly ordered to one's knees. A bust of Napoleon was then illumined in a niche in the wall. And so on. Great fun. You certainly shouldn't miss a visit to Tao. He is very wonderful, as well as rather famous, and if you wish, he can actually put you up in his exotic establishment. After Chez Tao, it is moving from the sublime to the ridiculous to tell you that there is also a cinema in Calvi.

*Le Camping:* There are a large number of well-run establishments around the bay, of which I presently recommend the Club Franco-Britannique and the Chalets Les Tamaris. And, since no self-respecting *camping* now wants to be without its Bar-Dancing, you will find several of these off the road hereabouts. The Lido on the plage (first structure as you proceed from the town) also caters to the perpetual-motion crowd, but no hand-holding nooks here, I fear, and the victuals are indifferent.

*Petrol Pump:* Two good garages, with repair mechanics, one right beside the Palace.

Founded in 1268 by de Loreto, an ally of the Genoese, Calvi is the customary Corsican citadel town, placed strategically on a promontory. It is today a spectacular seaside resort, becoming more and more popular each year. It does not have any sense of indigenous life, at least not one visible to the average visitor, but if you cannot move around the island it is as attractive a place to spend your summer at as any.

Since I have mentioned that Calvi is served by both boat and air from the mainland, and because it is particularly well-known, it may be that you will expect a larger town than you will actually find. Calvi is a *Sous-préfecture* of some two thousand inhabitants only, however, and you can easily walk all round it in a matter of minutes.

The "lower town," with its delightful waterfront ranked by a row of Dufy-like cafés and restaurants and facing the nodding plumes of yachts of all varieties and vintages, is surmounted by a characteristic Citadel.

This crumbling Citadel is worth a visit. A thirteenth-century church can also be visited and you will find a

149

hopeful plaque "commemorating," in 1441, one of the several birth-places of Christopher Columbus. Nothing in memory of Nelson's lost eye, however, beyond the savage scars of his cannon-balls on the dome of the church.

The great tourist attraction is, of course, the sweep of Calvi's sandy bay. And it is a sweep. Eight kilometres by local estimate. But I can't believe this since I have frequently walked all round and back without any effort at all. Still, the beach is of that order, certainly, a splendid fan of white sand backed by pine groves and occasional palms. Backed too, I should add, by a railway line (several trains a day in each direction in the summer) and by the set of French *campings* already mentioned. These last have got to be too much of a good thing, so far as I'm concerned. During August the inhabitants of these tents, shacks, and sheds inundate the beach and make it hard to find a quiet corner anywhere on it. There are water-skiing boats, and *pedalos* galore, and coloured umbrellas and chairs to hire of every conceivable description. Finally, as hinted above, the Gulf of Calvi itself slopes so very gradually that you are sometimes only waist-deep in water 50 yards out.

If the above again strikes you as negative, let me confer a rider on this chapter; the great range of ash-coloured mountains across the bay, still streaked faintly with snow even in July, are definitely under-written. These arid slopes, highly reminiscent of North Africa, turn every colour of the rainbow at sunset. Sometimes they slide into mauves and pale greys, or another night the whole grim backdrop will go a gorgeous shrimp pink, before fading

150

into the sky. Don't fail to watch the sunset light these mountains from your balcony in the Palace.

## FROM CALVI TO ILE ROUSSE
### (24 kilometres)

An easy and pleasant run alongside one of the most fertile areas of Corsica, the market garden of the island, in fact, known as *La Balagne*. (41) You leave Calvi following the line of the gulf and passing on your right the airport and sundry other military and municipal buildings of calculated hideousness. These are nicely hidden from the town, however, as is not invariably the case. You then cross a stream called the Secco on one of those bridges made up of loose wooden blocks so frequent in Corsica; I might mention that it is best to take these slowly if driving, as it's possible when travelling at speed to throw up a block and hit another car behind. You then start a gradual climb to *Lumio,* passing an old Roman church on your way into the village. Lumio, which you see twinkling at night from Calvi, commands a fine view into the first of the Balagne valleys.

Now, if you want to take a look at the celebrated Dominican *Convent of Corbara,* or the amazing hill village of *Sant' Antonino* (neither of which I take you to below), you should turn right, into the interior, at Lumio. However, there is an arranged excursion to both places from Ile Rousse, and the motoring up to Sant' Antonino is precipitous. Don't try it, as I did, with one sparking plug on the blink.

The roads into the hinterland here are not especially well marked, but they are breathtakingly beautiful and

---

(41) I propose a foray into this beautiful area, in Part III below.

surprisingly good as far as the surface is concerned. For Sant' Antonino, which you will see perched high above you as you approach, proceed along N 197 for $7\frac{1}{2}$ kilometres and then turn left at the cross-roads. This hill village is certainly worth a visit, if you can possibly manage it, for its thrilling view over the country, and sea coast, around. You can then follow on to rejoin the road you have left at about $1\frac{1}{2}$ kilometres from Ile Rousse itself. If you go this way, you will not only have marvellous panoramas opening continually under you as you drive, but will pass on your right the Corbara Convent mentioned. This was originally a fifteenth-century Franciscan monastery.

If you want to bathe on some isolated and lovely beaches between Calvi and Ile Rousse, on the other hand, keep straight ahead along old N 199 at Lumio. This will rapidly deliver you to *Algajola,* not a particularly interesting village but with a perfect beach no one has yet exploited; there are, in fact, two or three first-class curves of sand just by here. One has been discovered by the inevitable *camping,* but the others are generally deserted. There are a couple of hotels at Algajola: the Hôtel de la Plage, formerly the Martelli (tel.: Cabine d'Algajola), and a newer establishment called the Hôtel Capo-Rosso (tel.: 3). Both simple but satisfactory.

About five kilometres before Ile Rousse, as you begin to descend into the town, the granite quarry can be seen from which was taken the stone that supports the Vendôme column in Paris. You will then see the red granite islet, projecting into the sea and carrying the lighthouse, from which the town takes its name. Turn left off N 199 to get into Ile Rousse itself. There's nearly always a policeman on duty at this point.

# ILE ROUSSE

*Hotels:*

> Napoléon-Bonaparte (tel. : 9, 10, 91)
> Splendid (tel. : 24)
> Le Grillon (tel. : 40)
> L'Auberge (tel. : 19)
> Salducci.

My recommendations: As a matter of fact, partly because of the large size of the Napoléon-Bonaparte, which has 150 rooms, Ile Rousse actually boasts more hotel accommodation than Calvi at present writing. If you have enough in your pockets, I strongly recommend the Napoléon-Bonaparte, which is the only hotel of luxury class on Corsica. It is expensive but *very good value*—much more so than certain costlier Riviera emporiums I know of. Established in an old château, to which tasteful conversions have been added, this hotel has a first-class cuisine, small armies of service, a terrace, good hard tennis-court, and very comfortable rooms, the décor of which is sedulously Napoleonic. As I am not writing advertising copy for this or any other hotel in Corsica, however, I can tell you that the golf it everywhere advertises is a miniature course and that its private plage (at least the stretch where it maintains beach-huts) is inferior to others close at hand. All the same, it is a well-run establishment and, if you can afford it, an excellent one to settle at for a healthy family holiday by the sea. This is, in fact, much more the tone of the Napoléon-Bonaparte—that set by prosperous French burgher families, with lots of children —rather than of the *haut monde,* film-stars and the like. If you cannot afford this hotel try L'Auberge on the plage. Its manager, M. Chevallier, is courtesy itself and his cuisine admirable. The hotels here all provide the best

restaurants and *distractions;* there is a small cinema.
Casino.

*Petrol Pump:* the Hôtel Napoléon-Bonaparte has its own.
But on the way out of the town there is a large, good
garage, capable of repairs.

Created in 1758 by Pascal Paoli to offset the Genoese-
influenced Calvi nearby, Ile Rousse is distinguished by a
leafy square called the Place Paoli. A white marble bust
to the hero of Corsican independence rises in the centre
of this plaza, which is heavily shaded by plane-trees and
faces the sea. Here too, along one side, fruit and vegetable
produce is sold in a thriving market.

The bathing beaches, which string out to the north,
are much better than sometimes reported (especially by
the Calvais!). The sand is very fine and the beach, unlike
that at Calvi, is broken up into smaller circlets. Moreover,
it is protected from the winds which can make Calvi's
sands intolerable at times. Yet again you have here another
most gently shelving shoreline which means that you
have to wade out to swim in most parts.


## FROM ILE ROUSSE TO SAINT-FLORENT
### (46 kilometres)

Leaving Ile Rousse you follow the coast on an excellent
road until this drops into a bay called after the name of
the river that streams into it, *Lozari.* Here is another
perfect sandy beach, shallow and protected by trees at
the southern end, under the usual ruined tower, and
sharply shelving towards the far, northern point. No one
ever seems to bathe here, except on Sundays when the
locals use it, and the atmosphere, with the trickling river

154

to one side, and a few cows pasturing on the fertile plain behind, is entirely charming.

Once you have left Lozari you start climbing, and after a few kilometres leave the coast to cut across one of the most extraordinary landscapes imaginable, namely the *Désert des Agriates*. You do not see this as you first ascend, although the now wretchedly burnt hillsides here (for the environs of the Balagne were ravaged by fire a few years ago) prepare you in mood for the queer vista. Directly you reach the high point of the area, the *Col de Lavezzo* (312 m.), you start a sweeping descent towards the Gulf of Saint-Florent which takes you right through this rocky valley. Actually, the word desert should be discarded if it connotes for you—as it does for me—infinities of sand. This corner of Corsica is a sheer stretch of granite, acre after acre of it, a great uninhabited and uninhabitable expanse of what in abstract looks like a collection of giant macaroons, a Dali dream of pitted rock and serrated stone and pyramidal formations of gaping granite well labelled locally "Le Temple de la Solitude." It is one of the most oddly repellent views I know, frightening somehow in its almost total lack of life, of any flora and fauna at all. Here and there a few tufts of palsied shrubs cluster hopelessly, but the impression is one of alien hostility, of being on another, dead planet.

This impression is in just about as total a contrast as you could imagine to the first, ranging views of the Gulf of Saint-Florent when you descend. Here, once again, nature seems to have smiled. There is a sense of perpetual afternoon around this friendly bay, from the first glimpse of the reedy Aliso river which pours softly into it to the distant valley, filled with rose-laurel and oleander.

155

# SAINT-FLORENT

*Hotels:*

    Bellevue (tel.: 6)

    Madame Mère (or M'Mère) (tel.: 20)

    D'Europe (tel.: 3)

    Les Lauriers Roses (tel.: 14).

My recommendations: Both Bellevue and M'Mère—the latter a new hotel just behind the former—are good; both are situated a hundred yards or so out on the road north to Bastia and Cap Corse. Personally I always plump for the Bellevue because I think it perfectly carries out the atmosphere of Saint-Florent, which is quietly pastoral, perhaps the least Mediterranean in feeling of all the Corsican ports. The Bellevue is a small family hotel, impeccably run, with very good food indeed and delightful pergolas and terraces and even (so unusual on the island) excellent indoor lounge facilities. If you like the feeling of being put up as a guest in a quiet, easy-going house by the sea, this is for you. I heartily endorse it. The proprietress, who supervises everything scrupulously, is a delightful Dutch lady, now naturalized Corse. I have sometimes wished the service were a little less tensely " anti-gringo," but all things considered this is one of the most delightful places I have stayed in by the sea.

The Hôtel d'Europe is in the town and also quite good. Les Lauriers Roses is on the port with a flower-bedecked terrace for eating out there, and in summer it provides local guitarists.

*Petrol Pump:* A good service station right as you come into the town over the bridge—and incidentally watch the one-way traffic signs round the square here.

Saint-Florent is still a tiny fishing port, strategically sheltered at the foot of the Cap Corse peninsula. It was built in the fifteenth century under the Genoese and Nelson's exploits here are famous—he landed and reduced the local countryside. The port juts out under the shadow of a now ruined Citadel (to be scholarly about this I should perhaps add that it was ruined when I was last there and I suspect it still is). Fringed with those characteristically large-leaved French plane-trees (*platanes*), and with the peeling stucco of its buildings, Saint-Florent is enormously attractive but, as I have said, typical of what one has become used to. It is relaxing, rather than spectacular. An atmosphere of *fête champêtre* seems to emanate from those velvety, saddish meadows, and ambling cattle, and glossy river, behind it. If you stroll up the path towards the church into this valley of an evening, you will be reminded in mood of some early Renoir film. Not quite so lush perhaps, since the trees are mainly olives here.

As for bathing, the main bay extends right round from the port itself, a skinny strip of fine sand which is never crowded since *campings* have to date ignored this spot. Presumably they will come. The sea is very, very shallow. Excellent for children but a long walk to get out of your depth for grown-ups. On the other side of the town, as you drive out on the Bastia road, you will find at least a couple of sand inlets (as well as inviting rocks, of course, the sub-aqueous fishing off which is first-rate). One of these plages, to which you can turn left off the main road, is marked SANDSTRAND by the proprietress of the Bellevue, who runs a bathing-cabin and café concession on it. Not a flighty resort in the slightest sense, Saint-Florent has a genuine atmosphere and a character of its own which remind one once again how amazingly diversified this country can be in appeal.

# CAP CORSE

(From Saint-Florent to Bastia by the coast road
on Cap Corse is exactly 110 kilometres, or the
best part of 69 miles).

On leaving Saint-Florent in the direction I am going
you are faced with two alternatives: you can cut across
the base of the peninsula for 23 kilometres straight to
Bastia, or you can take the corniche road round the Cape
itself. You certainly should not miss the latter drive at
some point of your stay but, since it is one that can be
done in a day from Bastia quite comfortably, I thought
it best to cover Cap Corse in a section to itself in this
way, rather than stopping en route throughout it.

First of all, the road either way leads straight on out
of Saint-Florent and past an inviting bay. The turn-off
right to Bastia is clearly marked and takes N 199 off with
it. The coast road is N 198. Shortly after taking the Bastia
fork you come into vineyard country and the village of
*Patrimonio,* celebrated for its wines. You then climb the
*Col de Teghime* (548 m.), the site of the last battle for
Corsican liberation in 1943, which commands splendid
views over both sides of the island and, to the East, you
should—if the sky is clear—get your first glimpse coming
this way of the imposing outlines of Elba and Capraia.
The latter (which Paoli briefly invested) is to the left as
you look straight out to sea. And if you want to be
adventurous, you can branch right at this peak and pass
through *Oletta,* a pretty village nine kilometres to the
south. You may then keep straight on through the *Défilé
de Lancone,* another extraordinary Corsican mountain
pass, a strange sombre corridor hewn out of a precipitous

cliff-side. (42) This will take you down to the main road to Bastia, some nine kilometres south of the town. Otherwise you can simply continue on down from the Col de Teghime.

The route round Cap Corse itself is fairly justly celebrated. From Saint-Florent you carry straight on through the *San-Bernardino Pass* and soon find yourself back directly overlooking the sea. It is here that I have seen sand which can literally be said to be of a delicate pale blue in hue. It is also here that the underwater fishing is superlative. Try the *Marine d'Albo* or the *Farinole* inlet being sure, if you bathe in the latter tempting bay, to make some local enquiries about the prevailing state of currents first.

The entire road this western flank of Cap Corse is lovely, yet characteristically Mediterranean in configuration, except for the fact that it is heavily speckled with Genoese watch-towers. Nonza, however, which you soon hit, is unusual. This is an amazing village built on black rock which falls sheer into the sea. It is crowned by a tower and here it is that the fountain of Sainte Julie (whom I alluded to in my section on "History") may be seen. This sleepy, leafy village is too small to stay at but it is a pleasant one to stop at and stroll through. There are pebble beaches beneath you now and along here the road deteriorates as it passes through a quarry—of amianthus, of all things—the yellow haze of whose explosive dust hangs disfiguringly over quite a stretch of

(42) Some three kilometres or so south of the *Col de San Stefano* a rough side-road leads you to one of the most amazing chapels imaginable, the *Eglise San Michele* near the village of *Murato*. Of twelfth century Pisan architecture, this is right in the country, and by the nature of its coloured stones and marbles gives an extraordinary effect. There are also one or two genuinely primitive sculptings here.

coastline. In any case, caution is again warmly advised since the road becomes narrow, winding, and slow until you clear the tip of the Cape.

The *Minervio Point* gives particularly fine views over the coast and shortly after this you go through *Pino,* where I recommend the Restaurant Allard, and from which village a road cuts through *Luri* to rejoin N 198 on the other side; if you choose this way, which of course provides a slight short-cut, you will climb up the *Pass of Sainte-Lucie* and come under *Seneca's Tower* (also mentioned in my section on "History" above). You will further see, as you descend the other side, the cedrate gardens where the Cédratine liqueur originates.

Personally, if you have to make a choice, I would keep straight on round the tip of Cap Corse. As you come up to the *Col de Serra* (362 m.) you can get a marvellous sea view, with the *Island of Giraglia,* the northernmost tip of Corsican territory, beneath you. And about here I recommend you to turn off left some two kilometres from the Col down to *Barcaggio;* when I was last there the turn was marked only by a dilapidated and half-broken wooden post, of an unofficial nature, and most tourists had (I thankfully report) passed it by. Here you will find fairly good bathing off the beaten track and the Hotel of M. Mattei. A bit primitive to stay at perhaps (no running water on my last visit), but have a delicious fish luncheon there.

Back on the main road you roll into *Macinaggio* after a few more kilometres and hit the East coast proper. Here Paoli organized his expedition to take Capraia, and both Napoleon and the Empress Eugénie (later) landed briefly in the port. Frankly, however, I have always been rather disappointed by this stretch of coast from

160

20. Porto - Vecchio : the author on the Palombaggia plage.

21. Porto-Vecchio : the Palombaggia plage.

22. Bonifacio: the Marin

23. The inlet under Porto
Vecchio.

Macinaggio down to Bastia. This may be a purely personal and surface impression, and I should certainly hate to deter anyone from the run. For it is on this side that there are some hotels worth staying at. On the other hand, the bathing here seems to me over-rated and over-recommended—at least, don't imagine that all the *Marines* and *plages* in the nomenclature around here announce sand beaches. They do not. Several of these coves, like Pietranera and Griscione, are mainly rocky.

I except from these strictures the delightful *Marine de Meria*, four kilometres from Macinaggio, a sandy bay with a little restaurant as you come into it. The food at this café is only fair, but the people who run it are most kind. The *Marine de Sisco*, another seaside village, also has possible bathing and quite a good hotel, the Hôtel Giuseppi, with a patron of that name (tel.: 4). *Erbalunga*, five and a half kilometres south of Sisco, and supposedly "frequented by artists," did not appeal to me much, though it well may to you. A fairish restaurant here, too. And if you are a grotto hunter, there is a cave with fine stalactites and stalagmites called the *Grotte de Brando*, just out of Erbalunga.

A little further on still, however, is *Miomo*, or Miomo-Plage (although its plage is a pretty miserable affair after what you will have seen on the East coast); I mention this place not because its bathing is good, but because it is only five and a half kilometres of fairly flat-out road (speed "limited") from Bastia *and* it has a first rate hotel, one of the best of its size on the island. This is Les Sablettes (tel.: 25), a modern establishment with rooms with baths and balconies facing the sea and, since it is used for dining out by the Bastiais, an excellent if expensivish restaurant, supervised by the eagle eye of the proprietress, Mme. Corti.

With its tranquil, flower-strewn terraces and obliging service Les Sablettes makes, in my opinion, the very best place to stay in or around Bastia. Certainly, the next time I land at that town with a car, I shall certainly try to stay outside it at Miomo or Saint-Florent.

## BASTIA

*Hotels:*

Ile de Beauté (tel.: 3-29)
De l'Univers (tel.: 1-94)
La Chaumière (tel.: 5-35)
Riviera-Orlandi (tel.: 3-69)
Normandie (tel.: 4-22).

Also: Bon Goût — Corsica — Croix de Malte — De l'Aéro-Gare — De France — Des Voyageurs — Paoli — Du Palais — Luciani — Victoria — others are being constructed as I write.

My recommendations: Ile de Beauté. All these are uninteresting, commercial hotels, none of which has views a patch on anything approaching its counterparts in Ajaccio. But of the bunch I feel that the Ile de Beauté is the best. It is situated up a little hill of its own, where you can park your car, near the station. As a matter of fact, if you are shopping around and comparing prices, you can investigate four hotels in literally five minutes. The Normandie (which has no restaurant at present, though a blinking television set in the bar!) is directly opposite the Ile de Beauté, whereas round the corner you will find, in the Avenue Carnot, the Hôtel des Voyageurs and De l'Univers. The Ile de Beauté is the most expensive of these and Des Voyageurs the cheapest. I feel that the former is well worth the money: it is admirably run by one of the Mattei family. The same rules concerning full or demi-pension apply here, as in Ajaccio. But, as I say, the atmosphere in these hotels is one of business, rather than of pleasure. Do not let this put you off Bastia, however. You can always stay at nearby Miomo, as advised above.

*Restaurants:*
    La Concorde
    Lavezzi
    Pujula.

My recommendations: La Concorde, unreservedly. Like Ajaccio, Bastia teems with restaurants and it is here, in my opinion, that you will find the best food in Corsica. Rather than catering mainly for tourists, with supposed *specialités corses,* the Bastia restaurants have to keep in mind their year-round clientele of local business people, who are very much in earnest over their food. The cheaper restaurants can be found by strolling up one of the two main arteries of the town, the Rue César-Campinchi and the Boulevard Paoli (motorists should note the one-way traffic into and out of these streets). I know of at least three good restaurants in each street, all of which hang their menus up for inspection in their windows. The surroundings in these are simple, however.

Lavezzi in the Rue Saint-Jean is perhaps the most cracked-up restaurant in Bastia. It is unprepossessing from the outside and not many of the tables in its small rooms command that view over the old port which is often boasted for it. But the food is scrumptious. On the other hand, La Concorde is one of the few restaurants in the island where you can get first-class food, first-class service, *and* a setting with atmosphere all together. This restaurant fronts the plane-trees of the Boulevard de Gaulle so that you can sit and watch most of Bastia go by as you choose, and consume, your meal; with its gilded mirrors and scrolled ceiling this is just the sort of place I imagine Flaubert would have had Emma Bovary taken to by one of her provincial lovers. In any case, whatever you may deem the décor, at least it has its own quality and the food you will get here will be very, very good indeed. The two waiters are, for a change, culinarily knowledgeable and you can order practically anything you want on the *sur commande* list. Try the *merle pâté* or the *blanquette de veau* here. Try anything they have, in fact. You really owe it to yourself to make a dent in the cuisine of La Concorde before you go back.

*Museums:* Musée d'éthnographie corse. This may be seen in quite a short time in the Citadel, in the Palais des Gouverneurs established there by the Genoese in the fourteenth century (Bastia takes its name from the dungeon created at that time). Note Paoli's pistols here. Tragically enough, German mining destroyed a good part of the most interesting relics of the Citadel in 1943, but the Museum is worth a visit if only to take you through the delightful public gardens on the way back down to the Vieux Port, and to get the fine view of the coastline south from the Citadel itself. There is also the Eglise Sainte-Marie to see up here.

*Night-life:* Again, limited. The gone set can find a dancing place called Le Pigalle in the Rue César-Campinchi and at least three cinemas; I believe the Arinella plage now boasts the usual set-up for summer leg-shakers who want to jam it up all night on a pint-sized floor. But the restaurants in town seems to close rather before those in Ajaccio.

A great feature of the day in Bastia is surely the evening parade up and down the large Place Saint-Nicolas. There are several cafés which have tables out under the trees

164

here and at night each has its own band. Yes, these play at the same time! Fortunately, the square is so big that despite the stereophonic mikes each proprietor sets up for his songstress you can hear the rivals in relative comfort, even though the noise sometimes gets so fierce that the Bartolini statue of Boney in white marble (as Roman Emperor again) seems to quake and quiver at the far end of the square. All the youths in Bastia saunter up and down here in the evenings, stopping to sip aperitifs or just standing arm-in-arm listening. In the Bastia *passegiata* you will see girls with the tiniest waists in the world and lotharios escorting them with the longest sideburns ever. These hound-dog types carry no aura of Elvis Presley, however; it is—or was—just a local fashion *parmi les jeunes*.

*Post Office:* Large building on your right as you walk up the Boulevard Paoli from the Avenue Carnot.

*Banks:* see under " Currency " in Part I.

*Beaches:* Compared with those at Ajaccio, extremely poor. The best is a long, rather dismal stretch of sand, shelving quickly into the sea, called Arinella, a kilometre southwards out of the town. There's a bus service out in this direction but frankly this is very much a town beach, for local use, and not a patch on what you can find elsewhere on the island. Same with the Toga plage to the north.

*Excursions:* In the Avenue Carnot there are at least three small shops with signs advertising tourist excursions. One of these is the reliable Autocars S.N.C.F. As you are likely to have set up bus excursions for yourself before leaving, I won't pause to detail their offerings (v. my Appendix below). But, needless to say, you can find good trips round Cap Corse, to Saint-Florent and back, and so forth.

*" Essitac ":* 33 Boulevard Paoli (tel.: 2-04).

With a population of over 50,000, Bastia, the ancient capital of Corsica, is easily the largest town on the island. It is utterly different in feeling from Ajaccio. First of all, the environs are not nearly as beautiful; actually, you can overlook the setting from the villages of Cardo or Ste.-Lucie behind. Second, the new port is a large, ugly affair and dominates the first impression one gets—that Bastia is psychologically linked with Marseille, the principal market for the crops of those fertile regions around it, Cap Corse, the Nebbio, the Casinca. Third, the Bastiais are thoroughly independent and, if anything, more liberal and more sophisticated than their fellow-Corsicans elsewhere. Personally I love Bastia. It has a completely unselfconscious charm of its own, it is utterly untouristy, and if one has begun to feel conspicuous in the smaller Corsican towns, one can lose oneself comfortably here.

Bastia is virtually divided into two, the new and old; but, while larger than Ajaccio, the entire town can be covered on foot with ease. You will need neither buses nor taxis to get about it, unless you are in some way physically handicapped, of course. The new town, on the northern side, confronts you as you come in from Cap Corse. Here are the new port and the most modern buildings. In fact, large blocks of banal apartment houses are being flung up here as fast as possible, co-operatives which cost several thousand *pounds* to buy into per tiny flat but which are still heavily over-subscribed with prospective tenants, so an agent informed me. (43) Despite

(43) Should you by any chance be so interested, let me give you the names of the two best house-agents in Bastia: M. Michel Vincentelli, 7 Route du Cap, and M. Jean Agostini, Lion d'Or, Rue du Nouveau-Port. Both are close to each other; the former deals mainly in co-operative housing. But as one of them has put it to me, you have to be God to find an apartment in Bastia these days.

what I had read about the new town in Bastia, I could not really feel that this new building going on constituted an eyesore—as yet. Anyway the whole is dominated by the Place Saint-Nicolas, flanked on the west by the shadowy Boulevard de Général-de-Gaulle. (Motorists should watch the parking here; it's allowed in some parts, with others reserved for municipal authorities). The new town is also characterized by the two main streets I have mentioned above, the parallel Boulevard Paoli and Rue César-Campinchi, along which are a number of excellent shops, including some very well-stocked book-shops, by the way.

To get to the old town from this side, try walking to the south-east corner of the Place Saint-Nicolas, past the statue of Napoleon (the sea is east). This will take you down a street past a Lycée on your left, and you will emerge into the Place de l'Hôtel de Ville where one of the most thriving markets I've ever seen takes place. The foodstuffs here—fruits, vegetables, fish, cheeses, as well as some fascinating breads—are highly enticing to any interested housewife, and my own spent hours "window-shopping" here, while I perused a *Figaro* over pastis in a restaurant nearby. (44) Here, in this square, you can see the largest and most elaborate church in the town, the seventeenth-century Eglise Saint-Jean-Baptiste, whose twin bell-towers may be seen from the sea. And just by this church, incidentally, you will find the Rue Saint-Jean where Lavezzi's, the restaurant I commended above, is located. The entrance is, once again, modest, but the cooking excellent.

From here the Old Port is all yours. Directions in this maze of alleys, narrow steps, and flagged ascents would

---

(44) On this market square, let me recommend the mouth-watering *patisserie* of Mlle. Carmen Nicolai.

be ridiculous. And redundant. It's grand fun to discover one's own first dazzling glimpse of the blue waters of the Old Port through some blistered, washing-hung archway. The flag-stones here are famous, since they come from a veined marble with a particularly tough grain that shines brilliantly after rain. It rained a good deal my last stay in Bastia and I can't say I entirely agree with all the eulogies I've read on these stones, but they do have a quality of looking bright clean after heavy rainfalls.

The Old Port, with its motor-boats and nodding yachts, is surprisingly attractive, when so little has been expected of it from the majority of guides. Given this somnolent jetty in St. Tropez or somewhere similar, you would have the intellectuals of several nations in ecstasies of delight. Thankfully, Bastia is still unspoilt. To motorists, let me give some final advice in this connection. It is possible, and permissible, to drive up and down these flagstoned alleys of the Old Port; but as you will find on foot, it is trickyish. If you have a wide car, it is not possible. You'll get stuck for sure. Also if the fellow in front of you decides to get out and have a chat with his mother-in-law, it is slow to say the least. I mention this because on entering Bastia from the south there is a fork just as you pass the Citadel on your right. *Unless* you have a small car and want to risk driving upstairs, keep left here then, on the main Boulevard Auguste Gaudin into the town. This fork is not currently marked.

## FROM BASTIA TO SOLENZARA
### (102 kilometres)

N 193. This is a practically dead straight road down which you can do your 100 m.p.h., if you and your car feel like it. There is an establishment I stayed in at Solenzara which issued a brochure giving a time it took to reach the place by car that I simply refuse to quote here—it's an open invitation to suicide. But Corsicans expect to belt down this road at top speed. It is straight and, on the whole, very fast indeed. Let me issue a couple of warnings, however: first, in most parts the tarmac-adamized section of the surface (for it is not metalled yet) is too narrow to allow the passing of two cars. Consequently one or the other has to give way into the soft shoulder at the side—it often becomes a game of " chicken " as to which driver will hold out longest, as a matter of fact. You simply have to slow down considerably when edging into the shoulder and should accordingly allow for this for your own safety. Secondly, beware of the traffic just around Bastia. I have seen the débris of more accidents just leaving the town, where the road starts to widen and the local hot-rodders step on it, than anywhere else in the whole of Corsica. Better to be safe than sorry, as they say.

Driving southwards out of Bastia, then, you will leave to your left the *Arinella* plage mentioned above. If you want to, you can stop at *Biguglia* for a view over the long lake (or Etang) of that name. This 1,500-hectare lagoon used to be a port connected with the sea by a channel at its northernmost tip. It is now a stockpond of fish, allegedly richer in certain species, such as eels, than any other spot in the Mediterranean.

A few kilometres further on, you pass on your left the Poretta airfield with the village of *Borgo,* scene of one of Paoli's most devastating victories over the French, on a little hill to your right. But the road along here is the least interesting in the island and is freely acknowledged as such. On the other hand, I have personally found it less boring than generally expected. After keeping left at Casamozza (where a short stretch of railway also branches off to serve the East coast, and where the road becomes N 198 again), you pass by the rich *Castagniccia* area. Several roads lead off into this but my own experience has been that most of them deteriorate quickly; if you want to explore into the interior here, I urge you to select the roads marked as secondary (yellow) on your Michelin. Yet this stretch is admittedly unique in Corsica as not offering any ranging views at any point; even the sea is for the most part invisible behind the verdure to one's left.

Forty quick kilometres from Bastia you come, unimpressively enough, to *Moriani-Plage* which, like Solenzara further south, is being used for week-ending more and more by Bastiais. Moriani has a large expanse of characterless sand, a couple of hotels, several newish villas, and a petrol pump. North of it there is also a new *Hôtel pavillonnaire* or super-*camping,* a semi-circular set of cabins right on the beach called Santa Lucia Plage (tel.: San Nicolao 8). This is modern, clean, comfortable and fairly moderately priced.

From Moriani-Plage there is virtually nothing on the coast road—certainly nothing that might be Corsica—until you hit Solenzara, and I guarantee this is where your right foot will be nudging into the floorboards time and time again. Anyone in his senses, in fact, would cut out most of this stretch by branching right for Corte at Casamozza (a route I take you on in my next Part) and then coming at the coast again through Venaco and Vivario, at which point you turn left to climb the marvellous *Forest of Sorba*. This takes you along the flanks of Mount Calvi (1,071 m.) to *Ghisoni,* where again you head eastwards down to N 198; this has the advantage of leading through the *Defile of the Inzecca,* a mountain pass of terrifying sinuosity cut so deep into its gorge you have the impression of being at the bottom of a coffin, while a torrent burbles threateningly below you. An astonishing road and well worth doing, if you have the time.

Back on N 198 you will have passed on your left, between road and sea just north of Cateraggio, the celebrated *Etang de Diana,* another good-sized lake rife with tasty oysters. There are at least three more of these large lakes to your left before you reach Solenzara. I should perhaps also mundanely mention that, although you will almost certainly have topped up your tank in one of the many garages in Bastia, there is a pump at Ghisonaccia, 17 kilometres before Solenzara. There is no really good repairs garage on this side yet until Porto-Vecchio, however. Solenzara itself you enter after having forded the pleasant stream of that name.

## SOLENZARA

*Hotels:*

Mare e Festa (tel.: 0-10, 0-11)
De la Côte Orientale (tel.: 16).

My recommendations: The Mare e Festa is the most elaborate *camping* or *Hôtel pavillonaire* at present available in Corsica. There are comfortable bungalows and a central restaurant cum Bar-Dancing. The food is good and there is a large indoor dance floor, much patronized by week-ending Bastiais. I personally happen to think this set-up one of the most physically hideous places I have ever seen, but you may not; the décor is primarily Polynesian or, shall we say, *légèrement South-Sea-Island,* with garish masks and a mural behind the dance-band depicting some grass-skirted Amazons warming up for what appears to be a pole vault event, while an atom-bomb drops in the distance. The service here is excellent, however, and there are changing cabins on a private beach, and all that sort of thing. In fairness I must say that this is at the moment the best place to stay at Solenzara. It is to be found off to the left of the main road, clearly marked (and how!), as you come in; there is another hotel, the Auberge Pielza, five kilometres out of Solenzara.

*Petrol Pump:* On your right on the main road coming in.

Solenzara is a tiny village of practically no ethnographical interest whatsoever. All the same, it does make a convenient stop along this rather dull coastline and it has got good bathing. For this, do not use the Mare e Festa plage, but retrace your steps out of the town and turn right down a cart-track after crossing the Solenzara river. In a matter of a few hundred yards this will bring you out under giant eucalyptus trees into the Solenzara estuary; here are some wonderful beaches, and delightful sites for pitching tents also. The area was once malarial, but even this little sector was always healthy by virtue of its sheltering eucalyptus. Nowadays there is, of course, not the smallest danger in this respect at all.

## FROM SOLENZARA TO PORTO-VECCHIO
### (41 kilometres)

The first twenty-five kilometres of this run along the coast are immediately more interesting. Even so, I would always naturally counsel anyone to make the trip via the inland road up the Col de Bavella to Zonza, a magnificent drive which I detail below. Along N 198, however, you will find both fine bathing beaches and good camping sites.

The little bay of *Favone*, which you come upon eleven kilometres out of Solenzara, is first-class for both purposes. The road here is twisty and slower, but the surface satisfactory. You cross the Tarco streamlet and leave the coast at the *Tour de la Parata*, under another Genoese tower.

From here on, all the way down to Bonifacio, in fact, Michelin marks the coastal areas as mainly white, i.e. arid or non-verdurous. This is misleading. I have made mention above of the beautiful greenery around the Gulf of Porto-Vecchio and my criticisms apply most of the way down south now. It is nevertheless true that there are no grand forests here. If you have time and inclination, you can find delightful beaches off to the left of this stretch of N 198. Some of these roads are marked and some are not. Locals know them all and the majority of those I have personally tried have been eminently passable, since the sandstone here is easy to cut into. Try branching off left at Sainte-Lucie, after turning inland from the Col de Parata, and you will soon come to the magnificent bay of *Pinarello*, where there is yet another superb plage, relatively little-known. But there are other, even less frequented, beaches in these parts which you must discover for yourself!

## PORTO-VECCHIO

*Hotels:*

Chez Louis-Hôtel Holzer (tel.: 32).

My recommendations: This little commercial hotel, situated right on the main road, is virtually the only place of any considerable comfort in the town at the moment. Do not expect too much of it, however. The rooms are ordinary, there is no view, and the baths consist of showers in an annexe at the back. The place is used residentially by commercial travellers and local business-men and certainly provides a real glimpse of this kind of life for us Anglo-Saxons, who may have got our main idea of it from the French realist cinema; the dining-room of Chez Louis is a very different matter for this is a gustatory centre, in the season, for dozens and dozens of local campers and itinerant tourists, to say nothing of the vast masses housed in the seething Club Méditerranée to the south, who often drive in for a beano. In fact, the head waiter (a pleasant fellow called Marcel) told me that it was sometimes necessary to book for dinner a month in advance! It is much easier than this to get a room, however. The cuisine at Chez Louis is much better than one would expect from such an establishment, but it is, to my mind, disproportionately dear. There is incidentally an excellent rosé wine *de la maison* here, which quite rivals the Royal Corse rosé. Try it.

*Restaurants:* If camping nearby, you will find one or two places, like Les Gourmets on the way down to the Marine, and Les Platanes, which provide fair meals more cheaply than Chez Louis. Some of these offer rooms.

*Night-life:* Non-existent in the town which, by the by, has very poor shops indeed. A few kilometres out towards Bonifacio, however, you can haul into the Club Méditerranée or to the new Hôtel Santa-Giulia on the tip of the Golfe de Santa Giulia and dance *al fresco*.

*Excursions:* You can hire a local fisherman to take you out to the Iles Cerbicales.

*Post Office:* On your right down towards the Marine.

*Petrol Pumps:* Several. Moreover, next door to Chez Louis there is a good garage for repairs. The *mécanicien* here knows his onions. A good chap.

As will already have been hinted, Porto-Vecchio possesses little intrinsic charm, despite its suggestive name. At first glance it appears to consist of a number of fairly unattractive houses grouped around a main road, with no sea in sight at all. This is deceptive. Actually, Porto-Vecchio is the centre of what is to my way of thinking the finest area for bathing on the island. Unfortunately, more and more French are coming annually to share this opinion! But to date few English or Americans seem to have discovered it. Partly transportation difficulties, no doubt.

First off, the coast—including the beaches—is closely sheltered by pine-trees of the most sumptuous green. Secondly, the district is noted for its cork-oaks, strange, rather marvellous trees smaller than the Algerian corks and which, when stripped of their bark, give an odd impression of being somehow badly drawn, descaled, out of proportion. Thirdly, the wonderful sand here and relative ease of obtaining fresh water have made this Gulf and its environs a paradise for campers. I couldn't think of anywhere more lovely to spend a holiday under canvas than here.

A few hundred yards down the hill out of the town, Porto-Vecchio has indeed its own exceedingly busy port; long quaysides are continually replenished with stacks of wood and bark for shipment overseas. If you follow the road along here, however, you may find that the attractive-looking sand beaches you see have been fenced off, in the direction of the Punta della Varra at least. Try exploring to the north of the Gulf until you find what you want or, alternatively, take the road south to Bonifacio. Here I can give you useful advice.

Directly after crossing the five-arched granite bridge over the Stabiacco at the bottom of the hill leading up to Porto-Vecchio, and *before* coming to the secondary road which leads off N 198 to Figari, turn left. (There are other turnings, but this is the best to start off on). The track is barely indicated on Michelin, and indeed appears to peter out completely (just when it actually improves) after a collection of two or three houses on a sharp bend. In fact, this road is rough but perfectly feasible and used daily by French campers. At fifteen kilometres from Porto-Vecchio, or thirteen (slow) ones from the turn-off, you come to a glorious series of beaches, the first of which is called Palombaggia. Here, in summer at least, you will undoubtedly see tents.

The Palombaggia stretch is as good sand bathing as anyone, however fastidious, could ever want, though the underwater fishing is poorish. Large umbrella pines cast mauve shadows on ivory sand at which green champagne invitingly licks. The Iles Cerbicales dimple the water in the distance. Depending on your physical inclinations you can walk round to further beaches or motor on or just stay put at Palombaggia itself. If you take your car further on—and there are absolutely deserted stretches of sand to the south—let me emphasize that since the road winds, you have to go further than you think; secondly, you will notice barbed wire to your left, between the road and the beaches, indicating private property—a few cows will be grazing here, probably. The sand itself is *not* private, however, and you can take a track down to it.

It was here that my wife and I found the most happy atmosphere among the visiting French campers, who were all very definitely sun-worshippers. They say there is a nudist colony on an island near Porto-Vecchio, but I can't see its necessity, with the present healthy attitude to exposure prevalent among these French people. Most of the lasses had on bikinis they must have got into with the aid of shoe-horns or something, but I never heard a wolf-whistle once.

24.        Bonifacio: the cliff on which the Haute Ville stands.

25. Corte: Place de l'Eglise.

26. Monte d'Oro, landscape typical of the Vizzavona area.

27.        The Spelunca Gorge near Evisa.

28.       Evisa: looking towards the Gulf of Porto.

29.                    Sartène.

# FROM PORTO-VECCHIO TO BONIFACIO
## (27 kilometres)

This is a straight, easy run through pine and cork woods. Not until you reach Bonifacio does the road twist at all. Some six and a half kilometres out of Porto-Vecchio there is a turning marked off to the left for the Club Mediterranée. If you follow this (presently vile) track, as you are perfectly entitled to, you come into the beautiful *Golfe de Santa Giulia*. Here a strip of pine-sheltered sand separates another lagoon from a delightfully protected bay, to the south side of which rises a small mountain. The setting is superb for a *camping* and the Club has been inspired by it to give its bungalows Polynesian names.

Although you are not allowed on Club grounds, you are most assuredly allowed to bathe in the sea here and there is a little hotel with a pleasant terrace right at the end of the Gulf, called the Hôtel Santa-Giulia, excellently run by M. Paul Pandolfi. In actual experience, I have always found the officials of the Club Mediterranée most hospitable and, if you want to spend a fortnight in a really well-organized *camping*, with first-class equipment, you could not do better than with this outfit. The last time I was there, in fact, I met two English students and they were having the time of their lives. (45)

From here all that can be said for friend N 198 is that you follow it right into the olive area north of Bonifacio, and then down into the town itself. This you enter with the Marine on your right. As the hotels are here, you will doubtless want to swing off as you come in, rather than climb up to the town, which you can see above you.

---

(45) If you are interested, you should apply to: Club Mediterranée, 8 Rue de la Bourse, Paris, or, in England, to the same club at 139 Kensington High Street, London, W.8 (WEStern 1517).

# BONIFACIO

*Hotels:*

    La Pergola (tel.: 40)

    La Caravelle (tel.: 3).

My recommendations: Either of the above, both of which are on the Marine. The former, which faces right over the port, had several English people staying there when I last visited it and would probably be my number one choice. There are also a couple of other places, including the more expensive Hôtel du Roi d'Aragon (tel.: 25). But Bonifacio is not a place I envisage anyone, except artists, staying at for any length of time; hence fairly routine accommodation is what I advise here. Save your pennies for elsewhere.

*Restaurants:* There are one or two on the jetty and up in the Old Town, or Haute Ville. In the latter there is the Restaurant du Centre, but as there is nothing very special about these I leave you to make your own discoveries; Bonifacio, I found, is a great place for sitting over aperitifs, however.

*Night-life:* Nil.

*Excursions:* Here you have a must. The port, or Marine, where you will be staying, is a deep inlet into the calcified cliffs, resembling a fiord. This position, dominated by the outjutting Citadel, made the place practically impregnable from the sea for centuries. First off, to get a good view of the extraordinary horizontal rock stripings like so much puff pastry (and quite unlike the vertical crenellations of the Calanches), on which the Old Town is built, it is essential to see Bonifacio from out at sea. Secondly, there are at least three marvellous grottoes here rivalling the most talked-up sea caves of Capri — a group known as Le Camere, the Grotte du Sdragonato, the most distant, and lastly the Grotte de Saint-Antoine. With the pellucid clarity of its water against rocks ranging from grey to purple in colour, the Sdragonato is astonishingly impressive. The Grotte de Saint-Antoine lies under the southwestern point of the Citadel and you should get the boatman to take you right round the south side of this, from which the houses high above seem to cling to the cliffs with their very fingernails, and where you may see also the so-called steps of the King of Aragon (Escalier du Roi d'Aragon), cut up from the sea hundreds and hundreds of years ago—probably long before the actual Aragonese seige of the city in the fifteenth century. Thirdly and finally, you can hire a boat out to the very southernmost tip of Corsican territory, namely the Ile de Lavezzi, the scene of several shipwrecks, and where the habitual lighthouse now stands. In fact, the seas and winds here are still tricky and local boatmen will not put out every day for these islands. Ask at your hotel about these excursion boats. There have been so many tourists wanting to do these outings by now that they are thoroughly laid on. Do not expect the prices to be unduly cheap, however. And there is no haggling!

*Petrol Pump:* On the Marine.

Once again Corsica demonstrates its amazing variety in this extraordinary little town, which has been justly called one of the strangest in the Mediterranean. It is quite different from anything else on the island.

Founded in 828 by Boniface, Marquis of Tuscany, its Haute Ville is a remarkably well preserved sea fortress compressed on a limestone strip facing Sardinia. This *mille-feuille*-like rock formation is like nothing else on earth. Perhaps because of its proximity to Sardinia, indeed, Bonifacio seems in atmosphere the most Italian town in

179

Corsica. There is a vigorous feeling about the life around its Citadel and the populace appears to be more Genoese than French. They can be *extremely* difficult to understand. What is more, a South-Italian poverty seems more apparent in these washing-hung alleyways than in most of the island. Perhaps it was merely coincidental, but Bonifacio was the only place in Corsica where I was approached by beggars.

If you drive up to the Old Town I recommend leaving your car in the little park to the left of the main rampart-gates in; not only are the roads narrow as death as you progress upwards inside, but the small pebbles of which they are composed can be jolly treacherous in wet weather. Apart from one's natural pleasure in investigating the very real and individual character of the Haute Ville, there are three churches up here, two of which are certainly worth visiting: for the Bonifaciens are strongly Catholic and if you can get south for one of their local fête days (there are a couple at the end of August), you will see most moving processions of penitents, chanting as they go through the town. These are a well-known religious feature of the island, in fact.

Of the two churches, that of Saint Dominic was constructed in the thirteenth century by the Knights Templar and has an authentic Gothic quality. Apart from several pious pictures the High Altar is really rather fine in its way. The other church is that of Sainte Marie Majeure, with its loggia over the cisterns. Of mainly Pisan construction, it again is obviously very early and includes several relics, notably a piece of the Cross. Both these churches are quite central and, if you can't find them in the tiny Haute Ville, simply ask for the Rue Sainte-Croix. Believe me, your progress here is—as in any Italian village —closely supervised by several pairs of eyes behind window-shutters! It is usually necessary to get a guide to open the Church of Saint Dominic however. Simply inquire at your hotel about this and it'll be laid on for you.

Such, then, are the "sights" of Bonifacio, but my account does no justice to the real spirit of the town. The Bonifaciens are said to be a race apart, and I for one can well credit it. Bonifacio has an independent, autochthonous air and is definitely a place to see. In fact, you haven't really seen Corsica without it. At the same time, it cannot be said to be a tourist resort—gratefully, perhaps. Your bathing has to be done by boat. And don't forget while you are here how very easy it is to get over to Sardinia.

## FROM BONIFACIO TO PROPRIANO
### (67 kilometres)

Bonifacio is the only coast town covered here which you are obliged to leave by the route you entered on. Retrace your steps for a couple of kilometres or so along the Porto-Vecchio road and you will see a marking for Sartène to the left. This is N 196, which you follow all the way into Ajaccio.

A little way along this road you can get a marvellous view back over Bonifacio and right across a sea which looks as if it had been swept with a broom, right up to the first of the Sardinian mountains. But as you follow the coastline northwards it becomes slightly less interesting and offers little sand bathing, until you reach the hill where the road swings due north inland. Here, at an elevation called the Col de Coralli, you will glimpse the *Golfe de Roccapina* lying down to your left, whose granite lion I have referred to at the beginning of this book.

Right on top of the little Col a road leads off to the left, a cart-track really. The first few yards of this look fiendish (or did), but don't be deterred—here is another perfect plage to winkle out for yourself. Although the track narrows, it quickly improves and takes you down, after two or three kilometres, to a delicious bay dominated by a Genoese tower. This inlet is just east of what is strictly the Roccapina Gulf; it is little known and absolutely lovely.

Some few kilometres further along the main road one crosses a stream called the Ortolo. Here, off in the Cagna mountains to one's right (and not visible from the road), rears up the celebrated *Uomo di Cagna* (1,215 m.), a colossal rock shaped like a human face; do not attempt to reach it from this direction, however. There is a path leading down north-westwards from it towards a little village.

To your left, at about the same point, another plage is accessible off N 196 at *Tizzano*. But to reach Tizzano— as also another bay slightly further north called *Campomoro*—it's necessary to motor almost all the way into *Sartène,* and then branch sharply back. I have a soft spot in my heart for Sartène, indeed, but since you will find it covered in my next Part I shall not accord it any detail here. I should say, however, that the N 196 route I am following swings off hard left *before* entering the town proper so that, unless you plan to cover it again, you should certainly drive straight on into the main square, or Place de la Libération, and have a look around.

From Sartène the Ajaccio road (well-marked) winds down for a while on an excellent surface. Olive groves to right and left. Some nine kilometres or thereabouts brings you to a little bridge over the *Rizzanese;* I mention this because in my section on Corsican history I alluded to the prehistoric menhirs, or Stonehenge-like stones, which have been found in the island in recent times. Most of the best ones are in this south-western area and two may be seen just off the road near this river. What's more, there is another shorter road here leading off to the left to Campomoro. But if you keep straight on, you soon come into Propriano.

## PROPRIANO

*Hotels:*

Le Valinco (tel.: 69)
Le Lido (tel.: 37)
Colomba

My recommendations: Reluctantly, Le Valinco, which has an excellent position and good rooms over a fine plage. The Lido is along the jetty that protrudes into the sea, a dead-end which can be very noisy at night in the season since it is rapidly turning into a mass, or mess, of restaurants and garages. The Hôtel Colomba is a new establishment, under the proprietorship of M. Leca, offering roughly the same sort of deal as the Valinco. Then, at the far end of the Marine on which you find the Lido (towards the lighthouse), there is another camping called Le Corsaire (46); this is highly organized but less attractive than the Club Mediterranée near Porto-Vecchio. Further new hotels are already announced, to menace more of the coastline out in the Olmeto direction, where unfortunately the town inhabitants will persist in tumbling their rubbish into the sea. Of all Corsican seaside resorts, Propriano is quite the worst offender in this regard; hill-sides of stinking litter are growing annually around the bay. None of the hotels is very good—nothing even up to Calvi standards—but they are satisfactory if the weather

(46) If you are interested in staying here, you can apply to: Le Corsaire, 36 Rue de Courcelles, Paris.

holds fair. The Valinco has a fine dining-terrace looking right across the Golfe de Valinco, and the accommodations in its white-washed annexe are quite good. I recommend it reluctantly, however, in all conscience because the one time I was there with my wife, the place was jammed and the service at table was of the most cursory imaginable. Nor was it as inexpensive as it should by rights have been; the prices charged us for wine, in particular, were ludicrous. You find it, incidentally, by simply keeping on the main road to Ajaccio through the town. There is a private car park.

*Restaurants:* There are a number of these, of similar standard, all along the Marine.

*Night-life:* A number of dancing places at the above. Again, all of more or less the same standard.

*Petrol Pump:* Thanks (or not) to heavy tourist traffic, a number of these have now developed. There are good repairs garages on the jetty and, if you are staying at the Valinco, one just by the hotel itself.

*Beaches and Excursions:* The excellent bathing in the vicinity is what has made Propriano increasingly attractive to visiting *estivants, ressortissants,* and the like. More and more French families seem to bring their children there for a few weeks in the summer. There are a number of beaches. On some of these the sand approaches a gritty texture close to shingle. However, the composition of one or the other changes from year to year, as pointed out above. First of all, there is a huge plage as you look south-west, or dead left from the jetty. Then there is a fine sand beach right under the Valinco. A little further along in this direction, within quarter of an hour's walking, you come to the end of the Gulf itself and another vast sweep of sand, though with a rather desolate backdrop. On the far, northern side of the Gulf are several beautiful inlets to which you can be taken by boat from the Marine, if you haven't got a car; if you have a car you simply follow the main road up the hill to Olmeto and turn left on to a roughish track (D 157) just near a rectangular building which appears to be a power station of some sort or other. You can then tool along this track and pick your bathing spot, though in places you will have to stumble through the maquis to do so, for the road does not run absolutely by the sea. Nor does it take you *directly* on to Porto Pollo. To reach this distant, inviting point, you have to go inland a bit and cross the Tavaro streamlet and then come back to the coast again—and along here the driving is slow. But boat trips can easily be made from the Propriano quayside to both Porto Pollo and Campomoro, the northern and southern claws respectively enclosing the Golfe de Valinco. Underwater fishing off both is excellent. Moreover I need not remind you, if you have read my first sections, that the French Line boats put into Propriano and that you could, if you so desired, make your return to Ajaccio by ship.

Finally, road excursions are now laid on inland to two interesting spots, namely to the sulphurous baths of Baraci and to Fozzano. Near the Bains de Baraci, thought to be the site of Roman thermal baths, is a 36-room hotel, called Grand Hôtel des Thermes de Baraci (tel.: Propriano 14), should your rheumatism be playing up and inclining you to take the cure. This may be seen from the main road.

Fozzano is a tiny hill village with a superb view over the Gulf. It is noted as the birthplace of Colomba Carabelli, the heroine of Prosper Merimée's enduring masterpiece of 1840, *Colomba*. For Fozzano was the scene, seven years before the appearance of Merimée's book, of a celebrated *vendetta* between two local families whose houses may still be seen there. Merimée romanticized, yet universalized, the story calling the Durazzo family Barricini; in his novel indeed the conflict between modern liberal thought and unbending Corsican traditionalism is merely an intensification of what is constantly being dramatized in actuality on the island today. In Merimée's redaction Colomba's father is assassinated by the Barricini and the girl, bitterly committed to revenge, looks for this to her brother, Orso della Rebbia, who has just returned after a long absence. Orso's life in France, however, has widened his outlook and he finds the code of *vendetta* barbarically anachronistic; furthermore, he is in love with an English girl, Lydia Nevil, who tries to dissuade him from the act. Colomba persists in demanding blood-vengeance and Orso is about to perform it repugnantly, when the Barricini brothers themselves ambush him. Orso kills them with a *coup double* and so satisfies Colomba's honour without drawing down a galley-sentence on his own head. Needless to say, he marries Lydia in the end. The real-life Colomba, meanwhile, moved to Olmeto where she died at the ripe age of 96 in 1861; she was buried in the family vault at Fozzano.

But if you have time, any smallest archaeological interest whatsoever, and a car, you should certainly not leave the Propriano area without a visit to the Centre Préhistoric de Filitosa. This grandiose-sounding name covers, in fact, a few fields belonging to a local farmer where the earliest menhir finds have lately been made. These are quite fascinating and said to be among the oldest stone sculptings to have been unearthed in Europe. Digging at Filitosa is in progress as I write.

If you have a Michelin, the site is exactly by the arrow across the minor road due north-west of the name of Olmeto (Filitosa itself is too small to be marked!). You can reach the farm where the stones stand by continuing along the track D 157 to which I have made reference above; however, a more dramatic—and incidentally better marked—approach can be made by turning left at the hill four kilometres along the main road out of Olmeto. This takes you down into the strange little village of Sollacaro, site of much of Dumas Père's *Les Frères Corses* as also of the old Lords of Istria (the ruins of Vincentello's castle can be seen nearby). A short distance outside Sollacaro you turn sharp left and start plunging down a pretty bad path to the farm; lying along a hillside this track has been furrowed transversally by winter rains and can be very bumpy indeed. But as you go down, the rock growths in these luxuriant fields increase and with their savage character prepare you in mood for what you are to see. The name of the Filitosa farmer, incidentally, is Césari and his house is at a corner on your left as you descend. He charges a franc for entry into his fields, *which please respect*. M. Césari is the kindest of men and he will give you a deal of inside information on the sculptings, if you wish, in a French cheerfully peppered with Corse phrases.

The menhirs are in three groups and the Picassoid heads, staring at you from the central tumulus, are truly gripping. In fact, the faintly discernible figures—often with the ritual sword clasped across the breast—are so primitive as to be modern. In the fine group of upright stones, arranged in a semi-circle around a superb olive-tree, there are eyeless faces which bring to mind the work of more than one modern artist.

When leaving, you can continue straight on and you'll find that the track improves as it takes you round the coast, back to the main road again.

In general, Propriano is not a place that particularly appeals to me. The environs are, on the other hand, much more attractive than some guides lead one to believe; and I admit that the bathing in the vicinity is superlative. The trouble is that, although the port does have its place in the history of the island, Propriano is a fairly recent growth, under the impetus of transient tourists. It sometimes seems to me to have the worst of both worlds, namely the commercial acquisitiveness of a Calvi (without that town's pleasant resort atmosphere) coupled with the more sullen and complacent aspects of the indigenous Corsican village. But perhaps I simply struck unlucky here. I am more than ready to think so. My feeling is undoubtedly coloured by the fact that there are just too many people there in the summer now.

## FROM PROPRIANO TO AJACCIO
### (72½ kilometres)

The first few kilometres round the Gulf you will already have covered in order to explore the northern plages. From the turn-off to D 157 on your left, however, the road rises continually in increasingly narrow spirals. But the surface is good. Ten kilometres out of Propriano you come to *Olmeto,* grey houses hatched in terraces on to the hillside. Olmeto is perhaps a trifle deceptively attractive, as you may find if you take the right fork on coming up into it and have a look round its old town. But, as mentioned above, it was here that Merimée's Colomba died and her house may still be seen today; moreover, Olmeto has a fine view over the olive valley below it and over, too, the ruined *Castello della Rocca,* a fourteenth-century fortress erected by the great-grandson of the celebrated Giudice della Rocca (see my section on " History " above). From Olmeto on, the road runs through delightful olive groves and pleasantly pastoral land until Petreto where you should bear left, and where there is a petrol pump, should you require one. But there are, in fact, several along here, including at *Sainte-Marie-Siché*, which you soon reach.

This village (which I have pronounced for you above) was the cradle of the illustrious Ornano family who, besides presenting France with no less than three Field-Marshals, gave Sampiero Corso his Vanina of that name. Vanina's sternly patrician dwelling may be seen as may also the ruined fortress Sampiero himself built in 1554 after the destruction by the Genoese of his Bastelica residence. But there is yet more of Sampiero in this area.

Six kilometres further on you reach the *Col Saint-Georges* (747 m.) from which you start a lenient descent, gently winding all the while, down to *Cauro*, a summer resort for the quieter Ajacciens, and the coast. It is a lovely return, through idyllically green countryside, to the capital of the island. As you come down from Cauro, a branch road bearing back to the right serves the villages of *Suarella and Eccica*: just beyond the latter stands a stone commemorating the ambushing (by members of the Ornano family in the pay of the Genoese and furious at the death of their Vanina) of Sampiero. The great Corsican patriot died as he had lived, fighting. (47)

Lastly, I would remind anyone driving this way that at the *Pont de Pisciatello* over the Prunelli a few kilo-

---

(47) To continue along this road would take you inland to *Bastelica,* one of the ski centres mentioned above. Here— actually at Dominicacci—may be seen Sampiero's birthplace. The nearby *Prunelli Gorge*, incidentally, supplies Ajaccio with its water.

metres further along here, a minor road leads off to the *Pointe de Porticcio*. N 196, meanwhile, continues on a very fast stretch to take you straight towards the Royal palms of the capital, with the Campo del Oro airfield on your left.

Welcome back to Ajaccio!

# PART THREE

# INTO THE INTERIOR

My plan in this Part will be roughly analogous to that followed above. Starting in the capital of the island I shall proceed clockwise round the coast, describing four major forays into the interior, all of which can be accomplished in a short time and nearly of which are on pretty good roads. These seem to me the very minimum necessary to any real understanding of what Corsica means topographically; needless to say, I hope you will feel inclined to forsake my routes, here and there, for some exploration of your own.

## AJACCIO — VIZZAVONA — CORTE — BASTIA
### (153 kilometres)

You leave Ajaccio in the manner already described for the western coastline; but instead of turning left at Mezzavia, where the sign is marked for Calvi, keep straight on along N 193. You are now motoring right through the heart of the island, on one of its principal and oldest arteries.

As you will see from the map, the road follows the Gravone river through pastureland (only fairly interesting) for a while; you then begin to climb up to *Bocognano,* which is about 2,500 feet up and which you should reach within an hour. Set in superb chestnut groves, this is a delicious village, much frequented by those Ajacciens who find their city too hot in summer. In spirit Bocognano prepares you for a wonderful stretch of semi-Alpine scenery to come. There is a small hotel here, the Beauséjour (tel.: 4), where you can eat; if you do stop for a meal, give yourself a few minutes to have a look at the extraordinary gorges to the left, or north-west, of the village. The area (48) known as *La Pentica* requires some walking to get into properly, however. Even so, if you cross the Gravone and wander about this side of the main road, you will get something of the atmosphere of this old bandit country, where the lush undergrowth and diamond-bright waterfalls yield to the stark aridity of peaks rising up to as much as six thousand feet in the north.

From Bocognano to Vizzavona, in the ski-ing country already touched on above, the road spirals up and the air clears tangibly. You go through chestnut and pine woods and might easily imagine yourself in the Alps or, at first possibly, in the Harz mountains — certainly a completely other country from that you left on the coast an hour or so ago. One expects, and finds, hob-nailed boots here and woollen scarves and *Lederhosen*.

Personally, too, I find these chestnut trees the great glory of Corsica; they—and the ancient beeches up here with them — are among the finest trees I have ever seen. And if you intend to break your journey on this route I strongly recommend that you do so ten kilometres out of Bocognano at the *Col de Vizzavona*. Here you cross the central Corsican mountain range; in the old days, and still somewhat today, the inhabitants divide the island at this point in half, into "this side of the mountains," which they call *En-Deçà des Monts,* and "that side, or beyond, the mountains," *Au-Delà des Monts.*

(48) The word *piève*—district or county—is much used in Corsica.

# VIZZAVONA

*Hotels:*

Du Monte d'Oro (tel.: 6)
De la Forêt (tel.: 4).

My recommendations: Both are most hospitable. The Hôtel du Monte d'Oro is on the Col, i.e. before you come into the village from this direction, and the Grand Hôtel de la Forêt is off the main road to the left further on, just before the turn to the station. I personally plump firmly for the former; with its delightful timbering, checkered table-cloths, and general bucolic *bonhomie* it has the feeling of a Swiss mountain inn. The air is like wine just here and one has the sense of total peace, right in the heart of the countryside. The view over the road to the distant gorges is truly magnificent and what's more the hostelry is admirably run, with very good food and wine (the *patronne's* name is, appropriately enough, Mme. Plaisant). There are several other, lesser hotels in the village itself.

Vizzavona is a cheerful climatic resort with an average summer temperature of 57 degrees Fahrenheit (though it never seems nearly as cold as that to me in July). The air, which I have already commented on, is a real tonic and there are grand walks all round. Ask at your hotel about these if you are interested (and especially if you happen to be staying in winter or late autumn, when there is good rough shooting in the woods about): inquire for foot-paths (*sentiers muletiers* or *chemins de muletiers*). The Sentier de la Foce, off to the right into the lowering lariccio pine-woods a little way beyond the Col itself, is a well-marked and most inspiring one. It is also possible to hire guides for these excursions, if you wish.

The peaks or Cols around Vizzavona are fantastic, nothing short of staggeringly spectacular, in fact. To the

195

south of the village itself the *Pointe dell'Oriente* rises to 6,919 feet and *Monte Renoso* beyond that to 7,402 feet. *Monte d'Oro* to the north-west is of the same order whereas, behind it, *Monte Rotondo* reaches as much as 8,612 feet in height. These dramatic spikes are said to be the result of glacial deposits; their sombre ravines rise to grey pinnacles where, even in full summer, runnels of snow lie like sleep in the eye of the mountains.

I imagine—and I have no personal experience here— that the area around Vizzavona would be tempting bait to the professional climber. The amateur is constantly warned of dangerous spots by the customary skull-signs, I noted. Yet there are other Cols, such as *Palmento* and *Sorba,* which do not look nearly so forbidding and from the roads around which marvellous views may be had. From the Sorba mountain (alongside the road from Vivario to Ghisonaccia) you can on clear days see right down to the eastern seaboard. Then, not far across the road from the Hôtel du Monte d'Oro there are the little Ceppo point and the ruined Genoese Fort de Vizzavona. All things considered I encourage over-nighting here, if you do want to break your journey, rather than at Corte, historically important though the latter may be.

From Vizzavona you spiral down through the still vivifying air with the *Vecchio Gorges* to your left and the first hints of the *Sorba Forest* to your right. There are more fantastic stone formations off the road here, with the now almost usual animal shapes, rock balanced on rock in a manner to defeat even Pisan gravity, and so forth. You then reach *Vivario* (pronounced, once again, with the last vowel as a strong *u*). Set in such savage scenery, Vivario has always astonished me with its calm. It is under-written, though it is here that the fairly popular Ghisoni road (mentioned above) comes in. From the centre of the village, where there is an appealing little fountain to Diana, you can gaze out over a valley and spot several of the inimitably Corsican hill hamlets clinging, as if in some Cubist picture, to the sides of the mountains. In fact, I have motored along here and felt a strange, possibly primordial sensation of having been in this world before, although of course I had never seen anything like it in my life. Behind Vivario, forest mountains and grey peaks rise emphatically upwards. And there is incidentally one tradition that accords this commune the birthplace of the ninth-century Pope Formosus.

From Vivario the road descends and crosses the Vecchio and then climbs, amid rather more desolate scenery, to *Venaco*. This is a bit larger than you might perhaps expect, and there is a reasonable hotel, the Auberge du Vallon (tel.: 22). All along the road here to Corte there are marvellous views and one day I promise myself to investigate the strange, dark villages visible off in the hills up here. I should add, for motorists, that there are some bitter twists in the road as you corkscrew into Corte from this side.

## CORTE

*Hotels:*
    De la Paix (tel.: 22).

My recommendations: There are two others, both of which you will pass as you come into the town this way, but I advise the above, situated at the end of the Avenue Général-de-Gaulle a little further on, for its admirable cuisine.

*Museums:* Musée d'Histoire Corse, Palais National. Seven rooms dedicated to stages of the island's history. A relatively new idea, this building.

*Post Office:* Right in the middle of the Cours Paoli on your way out to Bastia.

There are also a number of the usual cafés and bars, of course, at least two good repair garages, one cinema, and agencies of both Air France and "Essitac" in the town.

Of all the inland towns Corte is probably the most important one to see. It can only be described as the heart of Corsica. The first time I went there I was disappointed because my initial impression was of the new town, which is characterless to the point of actually being ugly. As you enter from the Ajaccio direction, however, crossing the Tavignano and leaving to your left the old Franciscan bell-tower, you approach right under the beetling eagles' eyrie of Corte's incomparable Citadel. This craggy eminence personifies Corsican independence to my mind. Embodied in this jutting Churchillian jaw of rock, or Lincoln-like forehead of the landscape, a fierce pride reminds us that under Paoli (whose statue stands in the Place Paoli at juncture of old and new towns), this was the centre of the island, its intellectual as well as legal capital; it reminds us, too, in no uncertain terms, that such was the patriotism of the Cortenais under Genoa that the local women frequently swore never to marry, in order not to give birth to slaves.

If you stroll up into the Old Town, in fact, this feeling will accompany you everywhere. It is the repository of a people's faith, fortified in the town hall blotched by Genoese cannon-balls, immortalized in the Gaffori mansion where the wife of the Corsican General of that name (whose likeness stands before the house) withstood a whole Genoese siege single-handed in 1750, stiffened finally in the *maison natale,* just near the Citadel itself, of the future King of Spain, Joseph Bonaparte. If you do not, finally, feel that Corsican history exudes from all these old stones around you here, try a visit to the little Museum mentioned. Up in the Old Town, too, is the Eglise de l'Annonciation, an eighteenth-century church from which it is said that Mme. Laetitia (de) Ramolino, with Napoleon in her womb, left to accompany her husband, Charles, along the goat tracks out of Corte.

From the Old Town, dominated as it is, then, by the Citadel created in 1419 by Vincentello d'Istria, you come to a little belvedere from which are superb views over the Restonica and Tavignano valleys; there are passable paths down from here into the adjacent countryside. Behind you rise in fold on fold the green and granite mountains, against which the russet-roofed houses stand out in sharp relief. Somehow I always leave Corte with a feeling of distinct respect. It is not a town where many readers of this book, except painters, will want to stay perhaps, but its remotely aloof quality symbolizes the very spirit of nationalist independence, and this is where the "dark" Corsica, that soul of the island I have spoken of, most certainly begins.

From Corte to Bastia the road is still interesting, with stirring views until *Ponte-Leccia*. There are fascinating-looking villages either side, while under iron mountains the land lies like a fawn-coloured fabric, flecked with emerald. Over all the distant churches drift, the fingers of their enamel bell-towers pointing upwards to the infinite cerulean as if in some positive assertion of possession.

At Ponte-Leccia (where the old Genoese bridge has been restored) you turn right for Bastia. There is a petrol pump on the main road here. The Golo winds beside you under rocks and crags and eight kilometres beyond the turn-off, after crossing this little river, you pass *Ponte-*

*Nuovo,* the site of Paoli's ultimate defeat in his struggle for Corsican liberation in 1769, that I have already mentioned above. There is a stone monument by the old saddle-backed bridge. From Ponte-Nuovo you pass through *Barchetta* where there is a road off to the left to some historically interesting and well-preserved villages, dating from the early Middle Ages. If you hold straight on, however, you hit the main coast road at Casamozza, already described above; you turn left here and buzz into Bastia. Once again, be prudent, as the French put it, on that last welcomingly straight stretch into the city.

## PORTO—EVISA—CALACUCCIA—LE NIOLO—ASCO—LA BALAGNE

(kilometrage too dependent on side-trips taken to quote accurately)

If Corte is the most important inland town to see, this route into the interior is far and away the most sensational —after the Col de Bavella route described below. It is a matter of personal predilections, I presume, your mood at the time, and the weather when you make the trip, as to which of these areas strikes you as most spectacular. Certainly there is nothing like either in the neighbouring Mediterranean basin. For this reason I have included this excursion into the interior in my itinerary for a fortnight's driving listed at the back of this book. I should qualify this recommendation by pointing out that, if you have not got the time to make this detour from the coast and want to follow the magnificent route north to Calvi that I have already described, then you have a convenient second course open to you, namely to motor inland as far only as Evisa and then turn back and take the northern Ota road into Porto.

The road from Porto to Evisa that I counsel you to set out on turns right just before the bridge where the petrol pump is; this I have already located for you above. Despite the fact that you are now climbing up to what is the highest road pass in the island, the drive is an easy one, and not so slow as you might imagine. It is only 22 kilometres from Porto to Evisa itself.

Almost at once the road becomes girdled with forestation, notably (on the right as you climb) dense chestnut forests. Michelin, while indicating the subsequent fir growths clearly, scarcely does justice to these wonderful woods where you may walk about in perfect peace, meeting only the occasional rooting boar or frightened bird. At seven and a half kilometres there is a branch road to the left over the Porto Gorge to *Ota*. If you have time only for a rapid sortie into the interior here, this, then, is the road to take back on your return. The sea is behind you now and across the gorge (whose depths are not completely overlooked from this road) you see the jagged crests of *La Spelunca*. This bristling cluster of needle-like points seems to throw the final menace of the red rock district at you. Ota is a scribble of grey against the hills. It is a small village with a distinct character and, of course, amazing views. The extraordinary feature of the twisted rock formations on the right bank of the Porto are, to my eye, the strange natural criss-crossing of the rock; close to, these lancing peaks come to resemble the hatch-work of an uncertain artist, or perhaps the faceted distortions of some clever abstractionist. There are also the haunting peaks behind, between Porto and Piana. A few pines grow around the Spelunca mountains, here and there, but on the whole the contrast of motoring up shady lanes to Evisa with these stark bones of the earth, as it were, opposite becomes most acute.

# EVISA

*Hotels:*

    La Châtaigneraie (tel.: 11)
    Belvédère (tel.: 5).

My recommendations: La Châtaigneraie. Both these hotels are small, and the Belvédère is open only through the season. The former is on your left a few hundred yards before you reach the town proper and frankly the Belvédère, which is actually in the town, is more attractive from the exterior. I fear that experience has taught me to ignore this dubious advantage altogether in Corsica, however, and the cuisine at La Châtaigneraie, admirably supervised by a very charming lady, is superior. I ate in both places in Evisa and would say that both were adequate, and that there is a definitely cheaper price range available here.

*Petrol Pump:* Two—one on the right and one on the left, as you drive into the town from this direction.

Evisa is a quite tiny summer resort on a hill. I merely pause here since for those few of my readers who might be hikers this would be an excellent spot to headquarter for a while. There are good walks all around, more or less fatiguing. Again—ask at your hotel about these.

From Evisa one rises rapidly into the celebrated *Forêt d'Aïtone* (pronounced with the accent on the diaeresis). To give pine forests their due this is a superb grouping of lariccios, that species peculiar to the island which the ancient Romans used for the masts of their galleys and which, in more modern times, Nelson used as an argument —ineffectual—for England's retention of the island. There are miles and miles of these noble pines, some of which range up to a hundred and fifty feet in height. You can stop anywhere along here and wander to the brink of the gorge. The views are astonishing, across from black firs to threatening peaks and plummeting down to misty depths below. Hollywood really ought to shoot its space films here—in fact, they may have done so now for all I know! There is usually a good deal of timber felling going on in the Aïtone Forest and regulations concerning starting fires are necessarily strict. Even if you don't want to stop in these woods, do not fail to get out at the *Col de Vergio*, the highest point a tarmacked road reaches in Corsica and from which may be seen the dark shadow of the sea.

From this point on you descend into the district known as the *Niolo*; this isolated *piève* is still largely inhabited by some of the toughest and finest strain of Corsican shepherd stock. It is only recently, in fact, that the area has been opened up. It is laden with some of the very finest trees in the whole of Europe — chestnut and pine — and shot through with dozens of crystalline streams, several of which increase to waterfall-strength beside the road.

## CALACUCCIA

*Hotels:*

Des Touristes (tel.: 4).

My recommendations: O.K. Simple, but larger than you might expect. Perhaps not as cheap as it ought to be. If you are a climber or hiker of any kind and want to explore a part of Corsica off the beaten track, you should certainly stop here or at Asco, right across north from you. Calacuccia is about the same size as Evisa.

There are several roads out of Calacuccia which should in any case tempt you; to the right a good one takes you in just over a kilometre to *Casamaccioli*, a tiny hamlet situated over the Golo with a fine view across to the highest point of the island, *Monte Cinto,* which is 8,891 feet high. Here each 8th September the local festival of the Santa du Niolo is held; I have never seen this and won't pretend I have, but it is said that an image of the Holy Virgin, believed to have miraculous properties, is ported through the village streets in a chanting procession or crocodile, called *"granitola."* More than anywhere else in the island, except perhaps the Castagniccia, this is the locale of folk ballads, and you would be lucky indeed if you could muscle in on one of the *veillées,* held after the old sixteenth-century festival, at which local shepherds improvise songs to set tunes in the traditional manner of the true balladeer. From Calacuccia, too, you can make other stiff ascents, in the direction of *Paglia Orba,* say, which is 8,278 feet high to the east, or to *Capo Tafonato,* just next to it and slightly lower. Secondly, there is a branch of the main road to the left by the *Scala di Santa Regina* Pass further on out of Calacuccia, and this will take you on up to the commune of *Corscia.*

There are some amazing rock contours beside the road, as it winds down to the main N 193 which I led you along, above, from Ajaccio to Bastia; moreover, the perfume of this inland *maquis* densens in places until it seems to acquire substance and cling to the skin like an oil. This route you follow along the stretch already covered, then, as far as Ponte-Leccia.

Here I should like to cast a passing glance to the right, or east, into the famous chestnut district of Castagniccia. Chestnuts, it must be remembered, were once a basic food in the Corsican interior; today, those *marrons glacés* you scoff in Nice and Cannes will almost certainly be from here. So if you can afford the time, the road into this area from Ponte-Leccia (N 197) is worth doing and little known. And it is unexpectedly beautiful. At *Morosaglia* you can see Paoli's birthplace and his ashes (the so-called Musée Pascal Paoli) and a little further on get a magnificent view from the *Col de Prato*. At *Piedicroce* pause for an excellent meal at the Hôtel de France, run by M. Filippi and sometimes known simply as the Hôtel Filippi (tel.: 2). From here it is but a matter of three or four kilometres to the ferruginous or chalybeate springs of the famous Orezza mineral water (see my section on "Food and Drink" above). This has been going for a long time — a million bottles were exported alone even a hundred years ago — and the present thermal establishment is set among superb chestnuts.

If you do not have time for this side-swipe, however, you should fork left at Ponte-Leccia on N 197 which heads north-west towards the coast. A few kilometres along here swing left again up a narrow, rocky road which soon brings you into the renowned *Gorges de l'Asco*. Strangely enough, these are more frequented by visiting tourists than is the Piedicroce road, so be careful when driving. This defile is nine kilometres of infernal landscape which at each turn threatens to close its granite jaws upon your car, until it opens out and you gratefully glimpse the Asco grumbling far below. If the Spelunca section was El Greco, this is sheer Brueghel—the Brueghel of *The Death of Saul* or *The Conversion of St. Paul*, with the rocks rising almost artificially abruptly from the earth. Only here it is real.

## ASCO

*Hotels:*
 Du Cinto (tel.: 1).

My recommendations: So far as I know, there isn't yet any alternative to the above, which is a modest enough establishment open only during the season. But it has a good restaurant and I would prefer it to staying at Cala-cuccia, if pressed to a choice. The proprietor is the local Mayor, M. Guerrini, who also takes an active interest in tourism. The village, quite tiny, is a favourite with campers.

Asco is well worth the rather rough trip to get to it. Situated on the verge of the *Forest of Carozzica,* into which you may make delightful walks (some superb junipers here), its blackened houses are scattered among the rocks like the centre of some ascetic retreat. Certainly it is in places such as this — and in others comparable that you may turn up for yourselves — that you will find Corsican traditionalism most austerely, and enigmatically, preserved. It is again only relatively lately that Asco has been opened up at all.

Back on the main route N 197 for the coast, which you will have left to get to Asco, you proceed through the bleak valley of the Navaccia for several kilometres, gradually climbing to the *Col de San Colombano* (682 m.). At this rise the landscape opens out and you can see widely in all directions over the *Balagne* to the sea. Lozari, mentioned above, may be seen from here.

An excursion into the beginnings of this area, so sadly hit by fire a few years ago, was made in my previous Part, but here the whole of this " garden of Corsica," as it has been called, is laid out for you in all its amazing fertility. There are said to be literally millions of olive-trees here, and I can well believe it; moreover, the figs and cédratiers appear here at their best. After the Col de San Colombano you come rapidly into *Belgodere,* yet another village in which, from a distance, the houses look to be built cube-like on top of each other, and from which you may choose one of two routes back to the coast, depending on whether you prefer to reach Ile Rousse or Calvi. The latter road (N 197) is more beautiful, I think, since it winds high over the so-called *Haute Balagne,* is little travelled at present, and takes you through a series of charming communes set in a semi-circle through *Muro* to Lumio, which has already been touched on above.

The Balagne is beautiful, especially when set against the grandeur and gravity of the Calvi Gulf in the distance, with that ragged majestic sentinel of its lone tower hurling defiance across at the porphyry chaos of the evening mountains.

## SOLENZARA—ZONZA—PORTO-VECCHIO
### (79 kilometres)

This is sheer Dolomite country. The incursion described below is one of the most popular among visiting tourists and motorists are met frequently on the road. At the same time, if driving down the east coast as itinerized in my previous Part, it would be ridiculous not to take this road, and for that reason—because it is so very well-known—few prefatory songs of praise for it are needed from me.

The first part of the route, from Solenzara to Zonza, was in fearful repair when last I took it, whereas the second half of the journey, down to Porto-Vecchio, was surprisingly good. I made my last ascent while mist clung about the banks of the trickling Solenzara. Nothing more Wagnerian could be imagined than those lovely gorges up to the *Col de Larone,* the river rippling below and the first fingers of the Bavella forests menacing from the distance. Incidentally, one most lovable characteristic of Corsican mountain streams is their clear sand-banks; the Solenzara, which flows over the whitest stones imaginable, has several of these at the turns on the way up. I should also prepare motorists for a stiff climb—in fact, 621 metres up in 17 kilometres as far as the Col de Larone, and almost exactly as much again in the next 13 to the famous *Col de Bavella.* Close on 4,000 feet up, that is, in under 19 miles! Moreover, the road twists crucially, so relinquish top gear for good until you get to the Col de Bavella and keep one palm close to the horn.

The Col de Bavella is best at sunset. Then nature seems never to have been so anthropomorphic as in this tragic duel of rocks and pines. Overlooked by the pinnacle of the Pargolo (1,791 m.), this Col is a green, boulder-strewn pass where the pine-trees have been deformed by high winds. Some fantasmagoric battle seems to have taken place and to have left the natural world shuddering in terror as it passed on. The wind whines in the evening, lumps of red rock arise like so many assassinated animals, when suddenly you catch sight of the gesturing fingers of the *Aiguilles de Bavella,* mountainous teeth set in a giant's jaw. The first glimpse of these overhead should best be fortuitous for full effect but, even prepared for, it has a gripping intensity. And after the false dawn of those white mists I last drove up through, there was something approaching witchcraft in the sight. These Dantesque formations mark the torn dorsal mountain wall under which Zonza lies. Certainly the Col de Bavella is one of the most extraordinary natural wonders of the island, and one unlikely to disappoint you, despite all the superlatives annually showered upon it.

# ZONZA

*Hotels:*

> De la Terrasse (tel. 12)
> Du Mouflon d'Or (tel.: 3).

My recommendations: Hôtel de la Terrasse. The Hôtel du Mouflon d'Or (or Golden Goat) is a more pretentious, rather publicity-conscious place, down a hill out of the town to the right as you come in this way. It is far more expensive than any other hotel in Zonza, of which there are one or two.

*Petrol Pump:* At the main junction.

Zonza was strangely " occupied," when I first went there, by 40 or 50 French bicyclists in wasp-like yellow vests and purple shorts. They were about as far from the true atmosphere of this village as you could possibly imagine anything to be, and looked altogether inconceivably out-of-place. Zonza is peaceful, a bucolic resort facing age-old mountains, imbued with an immobility of centuries, full of the scent of peat and pipe-tobacco and, towards evening, of the bells of returning sheep.

Pine forests accompany you out of Zonza and gradually into the *Ospedale Forest*. It seems to me essential to descend into this, if you want to get the full benefits of the coming view out of the right hand side of the car. Climbing in this direction isn't nearly so scenic. But, as on the other side, the road spirals sharply, twist upon twist, and it's best to change down early and go slow on the bends, if you don't want smoking brakes.

Then, stop at the top of the village called *l'Ospedale*. If it is a good day, you will have at your feet a magnificent sweep of the entire southern plain of Corsica right out over the island-sprinkled straits to the first outline of

Sardinia, whose mountains dimly festoon the distance. It is the finest view of this part of the island possible.

There is nothing in l'Ospedale itself, however, and just under 20 kilometres of a fairly quick descent takes you back to the coast road (N 198) where you turn right for Porto-Vecchio.

## GHISONI—ZICAVO—SARTENE
### (99 kilometres)

A much neglected route (N 194) slap down the centre of the island, and one that would adorn your itinerary if you have already "done" Vizzavona. It is simply a matter of keeping left at Vivario and taking the road through the Forêt de Sorba to Ghisoni, mentioned above. Enclosed at the crossing of two deep valleys, Ghisoni is a tiny, terraced village well worth seeing, since it fronts two magnificent peaks to the south-east named *Christe Eleison* (1,220 m.) and *Kyrie Eleison* (1,534 m.). This central road down from Corte is known locally as the *"route des trois Cols"*—these being the Col de Sorba, the Col de Verde, and the Col de la Vaccia.

The second of these, near the *Marmano Forest* (recently ravaged by fires), leads you into the start of more splendid chestnut groves until you reach *Zicavo,* a small village lying at the feet of the towering *Incudine,* a mountain over 7,000 feet high to the south-east. In fact, the chestnuts are said to be physically bigger here than anywhere else.

The air at Zicavo once more seems of a marvellous purity, with the smell of spring perpetually about it. The village was the seat of the celebrated Abbatucci family (one of whose sons, a General killed at the end of the eighteenth century, has a square named after him in Ajaccio) and it boasts a small hotel, the Beauséjour (tel.:

7). I have no personal experience of this place, but it looked a satisfactory, if modest, establishment.

If you are inclined to take the cure, you could push a couple of kilometres off the main road to the right here to the *Bains de Guitera,* where there are two other small hotels and where the waters are said to be good for rheumatism. Guitera-les-Bains, unlike Baraci, is little known or exploited. Chiefly, however, Zicavo is utilized by summer climbers for the ascent of the Incudine, from which the view is reputed to be incredible.

From Zicavo the road rises through forested country until the *Col de la Vaccia,* when you begin descending through meadows interspersed with *maquis* towards *Aullène.* Here is another strange village, neglected of tourists; it is overlooked by the ruins of a castle built by Sinucello de la Rocca (see my section on "History" above). From Aullène N 194 crochets down until you begin to see the Rizzanese to your left. Here let me counsel a further incursion, or raid, into the interior.

This is to turn left off this road in order to take in *Sainte-Lucie-de-Tallano.* It is utterly beguiling and you won't see a single tourist there. Not as yet, at any rate. It has a sixteenth-century church dominating the Rizzanese and Fiumicicoli valleys and is replete with memories of the de la Rocca family. Altogether an unjustly ignored and delightfully sheltered commune. Finally, along the main road, you reach Sartène, already passed in my previous Bonifacio-Propriano itinerary above.

## SARTENE

*Hotels:*

    Sampiero (tel.: 3).

My recommendations: As above. An extremely small but pleasant inn. There is one other, not as good.

This is a sub-prefecture remarkably influential considering its size in the life of the island — I keep on meeting people from Sartène elsewhere and, for some reason, they often seem to be among the most sophisticated Corsicans. Whether this must be set down as surface coincidence or not, I don't know; yet it is true that this terraced town has truly kept something to itself of the quintessential Corsica. Sartène has conserved intact a really mediaeval spirit in its Old Town, with its uneven cobbles and stone stairways, its narrow black houses, and horizon dominated by the Convent of San Damiano.

The central square, with church and town hall, is leafy and attractive, and has at least two goodish restaurants on it. Today a wine-producing centre, the town's feudal aspect is best synthesized in the Passion Procession that takes place there each Good Friday. This is thoroughly authentic, a realistic portrayal of the stages of the Cross with Christ enacted anonymously by a local, in the manner of the Oberammergau of old. It is called the Catenaccio and, since it occurs at a time of year free of foreigners, it is still vitally indigenous.

Secondly, Sartène is—if you want to avoid the tourist hordes—quite neglected even in summer. As it is within easy striking distance by car of a number of lovely plages (around Propriano, at Tizzano twenty kilometres south-west, and the Roccapina beaches already mentioned), it would seem to me an original and convenient summer h.q. for the enterprising car-owner. I know that Sartène is going to be my choice for this part of the island before Propriano when I next visit Corsica.

Lastly, if motoring down to the Tizzano or Roccapina beaches in this direction, there is a famous prehistoric dolmen (marked on Michelin) almost equidistant between

212

these two roads, called the *Dolmen de Fontanaccia*. This, and the surrounding menhirs, are some of the finest quasi-Druidic remains on the island, but they are even more difficult of access than the Filitosa finds.

Here, then, in the heart of mediaeval Corsica we have reached a fitting point at which to take leave of this rough yet lovely island, the work of art of some smiling Olympian of old, at Sartène, *"la plus Corse des cités Corses,"* as it is fondly called.

There is no end to the writing of books on Corsica, but none has really yet surpassed, in the most general terms, that by the famous German scholar Ferdinand Gregorovius, who, in 1854, in his famous *Korsika,* summed up his indebtedness to the delectable island as follows:

> Corsica took away my cares, it cleansed and strengthened my soul; it freed me by giving me the first work to do, the material for which I myself had to wring from life and nature; it put firm ground under my feet. (49)

To the reader of this book, all I can truly say is — Come back again soon!

(49) My translation.

PART FOUR

# CHARTS AND APPENDICES

For all up-to-date information about Corsica apply to:

FRENCH GOVERNMENT TOURIST OFFICE,
Ministry of Public Works, Transport and Tourism,
66, Haymarket, London, S.W.1.

## ITINERARIES

### (1) A Two-Week Itinerary by Car:

AJACCIO — SAGONE — CARGESE — PIANA — *LES CALANCHES* — PORTO — *LA SPELUNCA* — EVISA — *COL DE VERGIO* — FORETS D'AITONE ET DE VALDONIELLO — CALACUCCIA — *SCALA DI SANTA REGINA* — FRANCARDO — PONTE LECCIA — ASCO — PONTE LECCIA — BELGODERE — *HAUTE BALAGNE* — CALVI — ALGAJOLA — ILE ROUSSE — *DESERT DES AGRIATES* — SAINT-FLORENT — *CAP CORSE* — BASTIA — MORIANI PLAGE — CERVIONE — OREZZA — MOROSAGLIA *(Maison de Pascal Paoli)* — PONTE-LECCIA —CORTE — VENACO — VIVARIO — VIZZAVONA *(Forêt)* — VIVARIO — GHISONI — *Défilés de l'INZECCA* — SOLENZARA — *COL DE BAVELLA* — ZONZA — *FORET DE L'OSPEDALE* — PORTO VECCHIO — BONIFACIO — SARTENE—PROPRIANO *(Centre préhistorique de FILITOSA)* — AJACCIO.

*Hotels and " Campings ":*
CARGESE: Camp du Carré d'As " Rocca-Marina "—M. Perrier.
(or) PIANA: Hôtel des Roches Rouges—M. Pandolfi.
PORTO: Hôtel Le Colombo—M. Milleli.
EVISA: Hôtel La Châtaigneraie—Mme. Santoni.
ASCO: Hôtel du Cinto—M. Guerrini.
CALVI: Calvi-Palace (Corsotel)—M. Biasini.
ILE ROUSSE: Hôtel Napoléon-Bonaparte—M. Chevallier.
SAINT-FLORENT: Hôtel Bellevue—Mme. van Hanja-Distanti.

SISCO: Hôtel Giuseppi—M. Giuseppi.
(or) MIOMO-PLAGE: Hôtel Les Sablettes—Mme. Corti.
MORIANI-PLAGE: Camping Santa-Lucia.
VENACO: Auberge du Vallon—M. Pagni.
SOLENZARA: Camping Mare e Festa—M. Gilabert.
ZONZA: Hôtel La Terrasse—M. Cavalli.
PORTO-VECCHIO: Chez Louis—M. Holzer.
(or) BONIFACIO: Hôtel La Caravelle—Mme. Rocca.
PROPRIANO: Hôtel du Valinco—Mme. Pantalacci.


## (2) An Eight-Day Itinerary by Car or Bus:

1st day:   BASTIA
              morning—town
              afternoon—environs

2nd day:  CAP CORSE
              morning—Bastia to Centuri
                    lunch at the Auberge Marcantoni
              afternoon—Centuri to Bastia
              (Centuri has not been covered above, and is well worth
              a visit; there is a tiny beach there of literally
                        rose-coloured sand.)

3rd day:  LA CASTAGNICCIA and ASCO
              morning—Bastia to Piedicroce
                    lunch at M. Fillippi's Hotel
              afternoon—visit to Orezza, Morosaglia
              overnight at Hôtel du Cinto, Asco

4th day:  LA BALANGE and LE NEBBIO
              morning—Asco to Calvi via the Haute-Balagne
                    lunch at Calvi
              afternoon—return to Bastia from Calvi, via the
                        Agriates, Saint-Florent, le Nebbio, and le
                        Lancone

5th day:  PORTO and PIANA
              morning—Bastia to Porto via Calacuccia, etc.
                    lunch at Porto
              afternoon—Porto to Piana
               overnight at the Hôtel des Roches Rouges, Piana

6th day:  AJACCIO
              morning—Piana to Ajaccio
               afternoon—town
              overnight at Ajaccio

7th day: **BONIFACIO, BAVELLA, AND ZONZA**
morning—Ajaccio to Bonifacio, via Olmeto, Propriano, Sartène, etc.
lunch at Bonifacio
afternoon—Bonifacio to Zonza, via Porto-Vecchio and the Ospedale Forest
overnight at Zonza

8th day: **ZONZA and BASTIA**
morning—Zonza to Vizzavona
lunch at the Hôtel du Monte d'Oro
afternoon—Vizzavona to Bastia, via the Vecchio valley and Corte, etc.

(3) **A Seven-Day Tour of Corsica via Europabus (no. 532): (50)**

*Monday:* Leave CALVI (Quai Kitchner) at 8.15 a.m.; ILE ROUSSE; DESERT DES AGRIATES; SAINT-FLORENT; lunch at ALBO (near ZONZA); LURI; arrive at BASTIA at 6.00 p.m.

*Tuesday:* Leave BASTIA at 2.30 p.m.; SCALA DI SANTA REGINA; arrive at CORTE at 5.30 p.m.

*Wednesday:* Leave CORTE at 7.15 a.m.; GHISONI; lunch at ZONZA; arrive at BONIFACIO at 6.00 p.m.

*Thursday:* Leave BONIFACIO at 1.00 p.m.; SARTENE; arrive at AJACCIO at 5.45 p.m.

*Friday:* Free Day.

*Saturday:* Leave AJACCIO at 3.00 p.m.; COL DE SAN BASTIANO; SAGONE; CARGESE; arrive at PIANA at 6.00 p.m.

*Sunday:* Leave PIANA at 8.00 a.m.; LES CALANCHES; PORTO; COL DE PALMARELLA; lunch at CALVI; arrive at ILE ROUSSE at 4.00 p.m.

The itinerary described above operates from March 25th to October 6th and costs approximately £7.

(50) Organized by French National Railways.

# CONVERSION TABLES

(1) **Measures of Length:**

| | | | |
|---|---|---|---|
| 10 centimetres | — | 1 decimetre | — 3.9370113 ins. |
| 10 decimetres | — | 1 METRE | — 1.0936143 yds. |
| 1000 metres | — | 1 KILOMETRE | — 0.62137 mile |

One inch is thus approximately 2½ cms.
One metre is thus approximately 3ft. 3ins.

One kilometre is thus approximately five-eighths of a mile, so that eight kilometres is roughly five miles, eighty kilometres is fifty miles, and so on.

A useful rule is: Multiply kilometres by five and divide by eight, to reduce to miles. Or again, since a kilometre is approximately sixty per cent. of a mile, you can make them into miles by multiplying by six and fixing the decimal point appropriately.

| | | | |
|---|---|---|---|
| 1 KILOMETRE | — five-eighths MILE (51) | | |
| 10 | „ | — $6\frac{1}{4}$ | „ |
| 50 | „ | — 31 | „ |
| 100 | „ | — 62 | „ |
| 160.93 | „ | — 100 | „ |
| 1 sq. kilometre | — 0.38611 sq. mile | | |
| 1 HECTARE | — 2.4711 ACRES. (The hectare is the chief unit of agricultural measurement.) | | |

(51) 1 Scandinavian mile—10 kilometres—6.21 English miles.

## (2) Measures of Weight:

| | |
|---|---|
| 1 hectogram | — 3.5274 oz. |
| 1 KILOGRAM | — 35.2734 oz. — 2.2046223 lbs. Avoirdupois |
| 1 quintal | — 1.9684 cwt. |
| 1 tonne | — 0.98421 long ton — 1.10231 short tons |

The kilo is the unit of weight employed when weighing baggage, etc., in French airports and the like; to reduce kilos to pounds, double the kilo figure and add on ten per cent.

## (3) Measures of Capacity:

| | |
|---|---|
| 1 decilitre | — 0.17598 pint |
| 0.57 litre | — 1 PINT |
| 1 LITRE | — 1,7598 pints (or approx. $1\frac{3}{4}$ pints) |
| 4.5 litres | — 1 GALLON |
| 10 litres | — 2 1/5 gallons |
| 50 litres | — 11 gallons |

Approximately one litre equals the best part of a quart—confusingly enough a French *quart* represents a quarter of a litre. U.S. gallons are larger than Imp. gallons.

## (4) Time Changes:

| | | | | |
|---|---|---|---|---|
| 5.00 p.m. | — | 6.00 p.m. | — | 7.00 p.m. |
| *London* | | *Corsica* | | Athens |
| Lisbon | | Paris | | |
| Madrid | | Berlin | | |
| | | Rome | | |
| | | Vienna | | |

## (5) Clothing Sizes:

### MEN'S

| Shirts: | British | 14 | 14½ | 15 | 15½ | 16 | 16½ | 17 |
|---------|---------|----|-----|----|-----|----|-----|----|
|         | Metric  | 36 | 37  | 38 | 39  | 40 | 41  | 42 |
| Shoes:  | British | 9  | 10  | 11 | 12  | 13 | —   | —  |
|         | Metric  | 40 | 41  | 42 | 43  | 44 | —   | —  |

### WOMEN'S

| Shoes: | British | 4 | 5 | 6 | 7 | 8 | 9 | 10 |
|--------|---------|---|---|---|---|---|---|----|
|        | Metric  | 37 | 38 | 39 | 40 | 41 | 42 | 43 |
| Stockings: | British | 8 | 8½ | 9 | 9½ | 10 | 10½ | — |
|        | Metric  | 0 | 1 | 2 | 3 | 4 | 5 | — |
| Suits and | British | 34 | 36 | 38 | 40 | 42 | 44 | 46 |
| Dresses: | Metric | 40 | 42 | 44 | 46 | 48 | 50 | 52 |

Absolutely no promises are made with the above table, since experience has taught me that such conversions, though "official," do vary considerably—in countries, and in individual shops. This applies particularly to the category of "Suits and Dresses" for women.

## (6) Tyre Pressures:

| Lbs. per sq. inch | Kgs. per sq. cm. |
|-------------------|------------------|
| 20 | 1.406 |
| 21 | 1.477 |
| 22 | 1.547 |
| 23 | 1.617 |
| 24 | 1.687 |
| 25 | 1.758 |
| 26 | 1.828 |
| 27 | 1.898 |
| 28 | 1.969 |
| 29 | 2.039 |
| 30 | 2.109 |

## (7) Fahrenheit and Centigrade:

| FAHRENHEIT | 0 | 14 | 32 | 50 | 68 | 86 | 104 | degrees |
|------------|---|----|----|----|----|----|-----|---------|
| CENTIGRADE | 17.8 | 10 | 0 | 10 | 20 | 30 | 40 | ,, |

To convert Fahrenheit into Centigrade, subtract 32 and multiply by 5/9; to convert Centigrade into Fahrenheit, go through the reverse procedure—multiply by 9/5 and add 32.

221

## (8) Film Ratings:

Since film sensitivities are based on so many varying criteria, it is very hard to provide any useful conversion systems. If you buy film in France of other than your usual kind, you should be aware that there may be a variance, however. For general photographic work the 20's correspond in most films bought; it is above and below this figure that the scales change from one to another.

## (9) Currency Conversion:

Since this is virtually the traveller's most important item of information, it is obvious that everyone leaving England for Corsica will check carefully on this before departure. As mentioned above, most travel agents and a few banks provide handy "Currency Converters" from time to time, The present *cours* for French francs is:

| 6d. | 1/- | 2/6 | 10/- | £1 |
|---|---|---|---|---|
| 35 centimes | 70 centimes | 1,75 N.F. | 7 N.F. | 14 N.F. |

# GLOSSARIES

## (1) Cooking Terms:

It is especially difficult to cater to everyone in this regard: some may consider the translation of many terms below insultingly elementary, while others may wish for an expansion of the list. In any case, here are a few handy words for deciphering that elegantly written French menu shoved under your nose in the average restaurant in Corsica and elsewhere:

| | |
|---|---|
| Aïoli | — garlic mayonnaise |
| Amandine | — with almonds |
| Baba | — yeast cake with currants |
| Bavaroise | — custard cream with gelatine |
| Bechamel | — classic white sauce |
| Beignet | — fritter |
| Blanquette | — " white " stew |
| Bouchées | — small pastry cases |
| Boeuf Bourguignon | — red wine beef stew with onions |
| Bouillabaisse | — substantial fish soup, served with whole fish in the broth |
| Brandade de Morue | — mousse of salt cod |
| Charcuterie | — cold cuts of various sausages (see above under " Food and Drink ") |
| Compôte de Fruits | — stewed fruit |
| Coquilles St. Jacques | — scallops |
| Courgettes | — young marrows |
| A la Crecy | — with carrots |
| Crêpes Niçoises | — pancakes stuffed with chicken |

| | |
|---|---|
| Cromesquis | — croquette mixture rolled in bacon and batter, and fried |
| Croustades | — cases of fried bread or pastry |
| Croûte | — thick slice of fried bread (n.b., the term *Casse-croûte* one sees outside restaurants indicates that snacks, sandwiches etc. are sold, in short, usually food to take out) |
| A la Diable | — with hot seasoning |
| Darne | — slice or middle-cut of large fish |
| Ecrevisse | — shrimp |
| Fiadone | — curd cake like cheese-cake ( see above under " Food and Drink ") |
| Florentine | — cooked with spinach |
| Foie de Veau | — calves' liver |
| Frappé | — iced |
| Fraises des Bois | — small wild strawberries (more common than the larger English kind) |
| Gigot | — leg of mutton or lamb |
| Au Gratin | — browned on the surface |
| A la St. Germain | — with peas |
| Haricots Verts | — runner or French beans |
| Homard Thermidor | — hot lobster with mustard |
| A la Jardinière | — with vegetables cut in fancy shapes |
| Aux Jus | — dressed with own juice |
| Lièvre | — hare |
| Macedoine | — mixture of fruits or vegetables cut to uniform size |
| A la Maître d'Hôtel | — with parsley flavour predominating |
| Merlans | — whiting |
| Merluche | — fresh cod |
| A la Mornay | — with cheese sauce |
| Morue | — salt cod |
| Moules | — mussels |
| Navets | — turnips |
| A la Parmentier | — with potatoes |
| Paupiettes | — thin slices of meat, stuffed, rolled, and braised |
| Oeufs Piperade | — scrambled eggs cooked with tomatoes and green peppers |
| Poivrade | — pepper flavour |
| Potage St. Germain | — cream of pea soup |
| Poulet à la vallée d'Auge | — chicken braised with celery and apple |
| A la Printanière | — with spring vegetables |

223

| Profiteroles | — fritters of choux or éclair pastry |
| Quenelle | — forcemeat poached in an oval shape |
| Quiche Lorraine | — a baked flan of Swiss cheese, bacon and eggs |
| Raie | — skate |
| Riz de Veau | — sweetbreads |
| Rognons | — kidneys |
| Salpicon | — savoury mince |
| Sole Bonne-Femme | — sole with hollandaise or white wine sauce |
| A la Soubise | — with onion |
| Terrine de Merles | — blackbird pâté (see above under " Food and Drink ") |
| Véronique | — cooked with grapes |
| Vichyssoise | — iced leek and potato soup |
| Vol-au-vent | — puff pastry case |

## (2) **Motoring Terms:**

Below are a few words, chiefly for parts of your car, that may help you when motoring in Corsica; I have purposefully omitted listing words that are virtually the same in both French and English (e.g. accelerator—**accélérateur**) or which would duplicate translations given in my section on " Motoring " above:

| to park one's car | — garer sa voiture, **or** (less common) stationner |
| check the oil | — vérifier l'huile |
| test tyre pressures | — vérifier le gonflage |
| clean windscreen | — essuyer le pare-brise |
| top up battery | — remettre de l'eau distillée dans les accumulateurs |
| clean sparking plugs | — décrasser les bougies |
| fill the radiator | — remplir le radiateur |
| brakes | — freins |
| clutch | — pédale d'embrayage |
| the steering | — la direction |
| charge the battery | — recharger les accumulateurs |
| petrol tank | — réservoir |
| springs | — ressorts |
| ignition | — allumage |
| distributor | — tête d'allumage |
| gauge (petrol etc.) | — jauge |
| exhaust pipe | — tuyau d'échappement |
| fan | — ventilateur |
| fan belt | — curroie de ventilateur |
| bumpers | — pare-chocs |
| windows | — glaces |
| mudguards | — ailes |

224

### (3) Road Signs:

Most French road signs are self-explanatory, since they tend to be pictorial. The three reproduced below are not, and they are important ones.

NO ENTRY

NO PARKING
(often grouped in pairs)

DANGER

## POSTAL RATES

In France these go by the gramme and seem constantly on the increase. At present writing the rates below are in operation between Corsica and England (the rates for postcards are for those with more than five words of message on them):

Letters                    50 centimes

Postcards                  30 centimes

225

# SCALES OF SELF-DRIVE CAR HIRE

These rates vary—upwards—from time to time, and from system to system. As mentioned in my text above, you should try to get a *franchise*, or free allowance, of 100 kilometres *per diem*. Some garages offer only 60. You will find a large deposit will be necessary, but this is not really an inconvenience since your eventual payment may be made out of it.

The Mattei "Location Sans Chauffeur" service currently offers:

|  | 7 days | 15 days | 30 days |
|---|---|---|---|
| CITROEN 2 CV. | 121,5 N.F. | 230 | 420 |
| RENAULT "DAUPHINE" | 160 | 300 | 570 |
| SIMCA "VERSAILLES" | 254 | 500 | 900 |

These rates should be carefully investigated to see that all is clear before signing your contract; Mattei offer only 60 kms. *franchise* at the moment, with a charge varying from 10 to 20 centimes surplus per kilometre consumed above the free allowance. There are sundry taxes.

Hertz Europcars, also mentioned above, are slightly more expensive, but allow from 80—100 kms. *franchise*, and I have always found myself able to get the latter figure over a period. Thus the current Corsican Hertz prices for a middle-priced car listed above are:

|  | 7 days | 15 days | 30 days |
|---|---|---|---|
| RENAULT "DAUPHINE" | 161 | 330 | 600 |

Other rates for other cars are roughly comparable and I should imagine there is not too much to choose between the companies who have doubtless, in any case, surveyed each other's prices pretty carefully.

## A BRIEF CHRONOLOGY OF CORSICA

| 260-163 B.C. | Roman conquest |
|---|---|
| 552 A.D. | Under Byzantine rule |
| 1014 | Moors defeated by Pisa and Genoa |
| 1077 | Papacy presents Corsica to Pisa |
| 1133 | Innocent II partitions Corsica, Genoa receiving dioceses in the north |
| 1299 | End of rule of Giudice de Cinarca |
| 1346 | Aragonese invasion |
| 1350 | Genoese reconquest |
| 1410 | Vincentello of Istria master of Corsica |
| 1553-57 | Sampiero Corso liberates Corsica under nominal French rule |

| | |
|---|---|
| 1559 | Treaty of Cateau-Cambrésis, at which France gives up Corsica |
| 1567 | Sampiero killed |
| 1729 | Corsican War of Independence begins |
| 1736 | Théodore de Neuhoff lands and leaves |
| 1739-47 | French missions of subjugation |
| 1755 | Paoli elected General of the island |
| 1768 | Treaty of Versailles, at which Genoa cedes Corsica to France |
| 1769 | Defeat of Paoli at Ponte-Nuovo |
| 1794 | Sir Gilbert Elliot appointed Viceroy |
| 1796 | British leave Corsica, which reverts permanently to France |

# A SELECT BIBLIOGRAPHY OF BOOKS IN ENGLISH ON CORSICA, WRITTEN DURING THIS CENTURY

Archer, Dorothy. *Corsica. The Scented Isle*. London: Methuen, 1924.
> Dated and rather pedestrian, but thorough.

Chiari, Joseph. *The Scented Isle*. Glasgow: William Maclellan, 1948.
> A brief, rambling book, full of life, by a Scot who lives in Corsica, comparing the island with the Highlands. Illus.

Clark, Denis. *The Sea Kingdom of Corsica*. London: Jarrolds. 1949.
> Excellent. Lavishly illustrated, and with an informative and well-written text.

Elwell, Charles. *Corsican Excursion*. London: The Bodley Head, 1954. Illustrated by Edward Lear.
> Limited. "Two of the most important towns, Ile Rousse and Calvi, were not visited." The 1868 Lear woodcuts, meanwhile, in the opinion of the reviewer for *The Traveller in France*, "represent some unknown island shrouded in mid-Victorian gloom, that is not Corsica." I entirely agree. Lear's drawings of the island were very poor; his text, in *Journal of a Landscape Painter* which can be said to have accompanied them, was much more stimulating.

Gotch, Christopher. *Corsica*. London: Peter Garnett, 1950.
> A brief volume by a writer who clearly tried to get about. Dated, however.

Hawthorne, Hildegarde. *Corsica: The Surprising Island*. New York: Duffield, 1926.
> For its time a most sympathetic travel-book by an American lady of leisure.

H*

Renwick, George. (With a Chapter on climbing by Thomas George Ouston, F.R.C.S.). *Romantic Corsica, Wanderings in Napoleon's Isle.* New York: Scribner's, London: T. Fisher Unwin, 1910.

Although dated by now, this thorough survey, heavily illustrated, was justly famous in its day and still bears re-reading.

"Snaffle" (Robert Dunkin, pseud.). *The Impossible Island. Corsica; Its People and Its Sport.* London: Witherby, 1923.

Post-World-War-I reminiscences, and how far ago they already seem, these charming anecdotes of boar and moufflon hunting.

NOTE: In addition to the above I should say that both *Go* (Hulton House, Fleet Street, London, E.C.4) and *Holiday* (Independence Square, Philadelphia 5, Pa., U.S.A.) have recently published full feature articles on Corsica in the respective countries in which they publish. Both are, of course, first-class travel magazines worth following.

Finally, as regards graphic volumes, the French naturally publish a number annually. Some of these, however, seem to me to have an "official" and posed quality about the photographs. If you want to get a really good idea of what Corsica looks like today, try one of the two German books listed below:

Guex-Relle, Henriette und André. *Korsika.* Fretz and Wasmuth, 1958.

Rossman, Alexander. *Anmut und Armut in Korsika.* Paul Haupt and Katzmann, 1958.

228

# INDEX

Compiled by G. NORMAN KNIGHT, M.A., M.S.Ind.

*For the more important references the page numbers are printed in bold type.*

Abbatucci Family, 210
Agriates, Désert des, 155
Air France, 32
  offices of, 34, 198
d'Aitone, Forêt, 202
Ajaccio: 53, **124-34**
  air services for, 32-4;
  banks in, 44;
  bus service for, 40, 129;
  cuisine in, 101;
  derivation of name, 131;
  hotel accommodation in, 69,
    105, 124-5;
  medical service of, 119;
  Napoleon's bust, 60;
  pronunciation of, 61;
  sailing to and from, 28-30,
    40;
  self-drive garages in, 38;
  shops in, 115-6;
  taxi fares in, 117-8;
  train service for, 38-9;
  yachting off, 91
d'Albo, Marine, 159
Algajola, 55, 152
Angelica, Martha (Corsican
  singer), 20
l'Annonciation, E g l i s e de,
  Corte, 199
Archer, Dorothy, *Corsica,* 227
Argentella silver mine, 146
Arinella plage, Bastia, 165, 169
Asco, 203, **205-6**
Asco, River, 205
Aullène, 211

Balagne, La, 151, 206-7
Baraci, Bains de, 185, 211
Barbary corsairs, 135
Barcaggio, 160
Barchetta, 200
Bartolini's statue of Napoleon,
  165
Bastelica, 90, 189n.
Bastia: **162-8**
  air services for, 32-4;
  British capture, 1745 . . . 58;
  bus service for, 40;
  cuisine in, 101;
  dress in, 88;
  house-agents in, 166n.;
  liberation of, 1943 . . . 61;
  Nelson in, 59;
  Old Port of, 167-8;
  sailings to and from, 28-30,
    31;
  self-drive garages in, 38;
  shops in, 115-6;
  taxi fares in, 117;
  train service for, 38-9;
  yachting off, 91
Bavella, Col de, 80, 172, 200,
  208
Belgodere, 206-7
*" Belle des Belles, la,"* 50
Biguglia, Etang, 169
Bocognano, 193-4
Bonaparte, Joseph, 60, 198
Boniface, Marquis of Tuscany,
  179

Bonifacio, 51, 91, **177-81**
  pronunciation of, 61
Borgo, 169
Boswell, James, *Account of Corsica,* 47
Brando, Grotte de, 161
Bussaglia plage, 145
Byron, George Gordon, Lord, 26
Byzantine Empire, C o r s i c a under, 51, 226

Cagna, Uomo di, 182
Calacuccia, **203-4**
Calanches (or Calanques), Les, 142-3, 145
Calcatoggio, 125
Calvi: 134, **146-57,** 154, 188
  air services for, 32-4;
  Citadel in, 147, 149--50;
  Nelson loses eye at, 59, 150;
  night-life in, 147-8;
  police in, 132n.
  road to Porto, 81, **145-6;**
  sailings to and from, 28-30, 40;
  shops in, 115;
  taxi fares in, 118;
  train service for, 39;
  yachting off, 91;
Calvi, Mt., 170
Camere, Le, Bonifacio, 178
Camping, **91-9,** 217-8
  Calvi, 148-9
  Club Mediterranée, 177
  Rocca-Marina, 136
  Santa Lucia, 170
Campo del Aro airport, 32-4, 190
Campomoro, 183, 185
Cap Corse, **158-62,** 166
Capraia, 158, 160
Cargèse, 91, 118, 135, **136-7**
  pronunciation of, 61
Carozzica, Forest of, 206
Carré d'As, Camp du, 136
*Casabianca,* submarine, 60, **138**
Casamaccioli, 203-4
Casamozza, 170, 200
Casanova, Danièle (victim of Auschwitz), 133

Casinca, the, 166
Castagniccia, La, 65, 110, 170, 204
Cateau-Camresis, Treaty of, 56, 227
Catenaccio, the (Passion play), 212
Cateraggio, 171
Cauro, 189
Centuri, 218
Cerbicales, Iles, 176
Césari, Mons. (farmer), **187**
Cesari-Rocca, Colonna **de, et** Louis Villat, *Histoire de Corse,* 66n.
Charles of Austria, Archduke, 105
Chiari, Joseph, *The Scented Isle,* 227
Chioni Gulf, 138
Christie Eleison peak, 210
Cinarca, Giudice de, 54, 135, 226
Cinto, Monte, 204
Clark, Denis, *The Sea Kingdom of Corsica,* 227
Columbus, Christopher, 150
Compagnie Générale Transatlantique, 28
  offices of, 31
Coralli, Col de, 181
Corbara Convent, 151, 152
Corscia, 204
Corse, Cap, **158-62,** 166
Corse language, 61, 63
Corte (ancient capital), 20, 77, 196, **197-9**
  citadel at, 54;
  University of, 58
Costantini, Simone, *La Gastronomie Corse,* 102
Croix, Col de la, 145

Dalida (Corsican singer), 64
Daudet, Alphonse, 131, 133
Désert des Agriates, 155
Diana, Etang de, 107, 171
*Dio Vi Salvi Regina* (national anthem), 20
Dominicacci, 55, 189n.

Doria, Andrea (Genoese commander), 56
Dumas, Alexandre (Père), *Les Frères Corses,* 187

Eccica, 189
Edward VII, King, 105, 131
Elliot, Sir Gilbert (Earl of Minto), 59, 227
Elwell, Charles, *Corsican Excursion,* 227
Erbalunga, 60, 161
Escalier de Roi d'Aragon, 179
d'Esigna, Forêt, 94
"Essitac," 127, 130, 165, 198
Eugénie, Empress, 160
Evisa, 77, 107, 200-1, **202-3**
*Evocation de la Corse* (disc), **20**

Fango River, 146
Farinole plage, 159
Favone Bay, 173
Fermor, Patrick Leigh, *Mani,* 137
Ferrandi, *La Rennaissance de la Corse,* 26
Fesch, Cardinal, 60, 127
Ficajola plage, Piana, 141-2
Filitosa, 50
    Centre Préhistorique de, 186-7
Formosus, Pope, 197
Fozzano, 185-6
France, Corsica part of, 54, 56, 58, 59-61
"French Line," the, 28, 185

Gaffori, General, 198
Genoa, Corsica under, 52-8, 59, 198, 226
Genoese round towers, 53, 133, 135, 138, 159, 182
Ghisonaccia, 171
Ghisoni, 170, 210
Giraglia, Island of, 160
Girolata Gulf, 82, 146
Golo, River, 199

Gotch, Christopher, *Corsica,* 227
Grande Sanguinaire, 133
Gregorovius, Ferdinand, *Korsica,* 213
Griscione plage, Cap Gorse, 161
Guex-Relle, Henriette u n d André, *Korsica,* 228
Gugliemo de Cinarca, 54
Guitera-les-Bains, 211

Hawthorne, Hildegarde, *Corsica, the Surprising Island,* 227
Hood, Admiral, 59
Hotels: **67-72,** 217-8
    Ajaccio, 69, 105, 124-5;
    Algajola, 152;
    Asco, 205-6;
    Barcaggio, 160;
    Bastia, 162-3;
    Bocognano, 194;
    Bonifacio, 178;
    Calacuccia, 203;
    Calvi, 146-7;
    Cargèse, 136
    Corte, 197;
    Evisa, 202;
    Ile Rousse, 153-4;
    Miomo, 161;
    Piana, 139
    Piedicroce, 205;
    Porto, 144;
    Porto-Vecchio, 173-4;
    Propriano, 183-4;
    Saint-Florent, 156;
    Santa-Giulia, 177;
    Sartène, 211;
    Sisco, 161;
    Solenzara, 171-2;
    Venaco, 197;
    Vizzavona, 195, 196;
    Zicavo, 210-1;
    Zonza, 209

(l') Ile Rousse, 91, **152-4**
luxury hotel at, 68, 153;
sailings to and from, 28-30, 40

Incudine, Mt., 210
Innocent II, Pope, 53, 226
Inzecca, Defile of the, 171

Julie, Sainte (Corsican Martyr), 51, 159

Kalliste (Greek for Corsica), 50

Lancone, Défilé de, 158
Larone, Col de, 207, 208
Lava, Gulf of, 134
Lavezzi, Ile de, 179
Lavezzo, Col de, 155
Lignaggia Gulf, 82
Lion of Roccapina, the, 26, 181
Listincone, Col de, 134
Loreto, de (founder of Calvi), 149
Louis XVI, King, 59
Lozari, 154-5, 206
Lumio, 151
Luri, 47n., 160

Macinaggio, 160-1
Maquis (or macchia), the, 24-5
Mare e Festa plage, Solenzara, 172
Marmano Forest, 210
Mathieu, *Mémoires de l'Académie Celtique,* 49
Melito, Miot de, 60
Menhirs found in Corsica, 50, 182-3, 186-7, 213
Meria, Marine de, 161
Merimée, Prosper, 49
  his *Colomba,* 185-6
Mezzo Mare, 133
Minervio Point, 160
Miomo, 161-2, 163
Molino-Bianco vineyard, 108
Moriani, 170
Morosaglia, 204-5;
Museums:
  Ajaccio, **126-8;**
  Bastia, 164;
  Corte, 197, 198;
  Morosaglia, 205

Mussolini, Benito, 60-1

Napoleon, I, Emperor, 24, 47-8, 60, 160, 199
  birth-place of, 48, 59, 126-7
  statue of, 165, 167
Napoléon-Bonaparte Hôtel, Ile Rousse, 68, 153-4
Nebbio, the, 166
Nelson, Captain Horatio, **59-60,** 150, 157, 202
Neuhoff, Théodore de, 51, 57-8, 227
Niolo, Le, 203
Nonza, 51, 100, 159

Oletta, 158
Olmeto, 183, 185, 186, 188-9
Orezza springs, 110, 205
Oriente, Pointe dell', 196
d'Ornano, Vanina, 56, 189
Ornano family, 189
d'Oro, Monte, 196
l'Ospedale, 209-10
Ospedale Forest, 209
Ota, 201

Paglia Orba, 204
Palmarella, Col de, 145-6
Palombaggia, 176
Paoli, Gen. Pascal, 25, 47-8, 51-2, 55-6, **58-9,** 154, 227
  birth-place of, 205
  "Italian patriot," 60
  military exploits of, 158, 160, 169, 200;
  pistols of, 164
  statue of, Corte, 198
Parata, Col de, 173
Pargolo pinnacle, 208
Partinello, 145
Pasqualine, Andrea, *Il Martirio della Corsica,* 60n.
Patrimonio vineyard, 108, 158
Pentica, La, 194
Piana, **139-42**
Piedicroce, 205
Pietranera plage, 161
Pinarello Bay, 173

Pino, 160
Pisa, Corsica under, 52, 53, 54, 226
Pisciatello, Pont de, 189
Pliny on Corsica, 51
Ponte-Leccia, 199, 204, 205
Ponte Nuovo, 59, 199-200, 227
Poretta airport, 32-4, 169
Porretone vineyard, 108
Porticcio, 130
Porto, 91, 103, **143-5**, 200-1
    road from Calvi, 81, **145-6**, 200
Porto gorge, 201
Porto Pollo, 185
Porto-Vecchio, 51, 79, 100, **173-6**, 207
    coquilles from, 104-5;
    yachting off, 91
Portus Syracusanus, 50-1
Prato, Col de, 205
Propriano, 103, 144, **183-8**
    sailings to and from, 28-9, 40;
    taxi fares in, 118;
    yachting off, 91
Prunelli, River, 189 (&n.)


Ramolino, Mme. de (Napoleon's mother), 199
Renoso, Monte, 196
Renwick, George, *Romantic Corsica*, 228
Restaurants:
    Ajaccio, 125-6;
    Bastia, 163-4;
    Bonifacio, 178;
    Erbalunga, 161;
    Meria, 161;
    Piana, 141;
    Pino, 160;
    Porto, 144;
    Porto-Vecchio, 174;
    Propriano, 184
Revellata Point, 146
Ricardo plage, 129-30
Rizzanese River, 182-3, 211
Rocca:
    Castello della, 188;
    Giudice della, 54, 189
Rocca, Toni (singer), 20n.

Rocca-Marina, 136
Roccapina, the Lion of, 26, 181
Roccapina Gulf, 182, 212
Roches Rouges Hôtel, Piana, 138-40
Romanetti, Nonce (bandit), 134
Rossman, Alexander, *Anmut und Armut in Korsica,* 228
Rotondo, Monte, 196
Rousse, Ile, see Ile Rousse
Rousseau, Jean Jacques, 58


Sagone, 135-6
    Golfe de, 134-5
Saint-Antoine, Grotte de, Bonifacio, 179
St. Dominic's Church Bonifacio, 180, 181
Saint-Florent, 58, 59, 91, 156-8
    plage near, 99
Saint-Florent Gulf, 155
Saint-Georges, Col, 189
*Saint-Jean-Baptiste* c h u r c h, Bastia, 167
Ste. Catherine airport, 32-3
Sainte-Lucie, Pass of, 160
Sainte-Lucie-de-Tallano, 211
Ste. Marie Majeure, Church of, Bonifacio, 180
Sainte-Marie-Siché, 61, 189
Salario Fountain, 131-2
Sampiero da Bastelica, 47, 52, 55-6 90, 226-7
    death of, 189
San-Bastiano, Col de, 134
San-Bernardino Pass, 159
San Colombano, Col de, 206
Sandstrand plage, Saint-Florent, 157
Sanguinaires, Iles, 133
Sanguinaires, Tour de, 53-4
San Michele chapel, 159n.
Sant' Antonino, 151-2
Santa Giulia, Golfe de, 101, 177
Santa Manza, 91
Sardinia, Corsica's relationship with, 51, 179

Sartène, 77, 181, 182, **211-3**
  Passion Procession at, 212
Sdregonato, Grotte de, Bonifacio, 178-9
Seal Cave, Calvi, 146
Secca, La (reef off Porto), 145
Seneca's exile in Corsica, 47
Seneca's Tower, Luri, 47n., 160
Sinucello de la Rocca, 54, 211
Sisco, 161.
"Snaffle" (Robert Dunkin, pseud.), *The Impossible Island*, 228
Solenzara, 169, 170, **171-2**, 207
Solenzara, River, 207-8
Sollacaro, 187
*Songs of Corsica*, 20
Sorba, Mt., 196, 210
Sorba Forest, 170, 196, 210
Spelunca, La, 144, 201, 205

Tafonato, Capo, 204
Teghime, Col de, 158, 159
"Temple de la Solitude, Le," 155
Théodore de Neuhoff, King, 51, 57-8, 227
*This is Corsica* (song), 20n.
Tirrenia Steamship Service, 31, 41
Tizzano, 182, 212

Toga plage, Bastia, 165
Tuscany, Boniface, Marquis of, 179
*Two Companions, The* (film), 145

Vaccia, Col de la, 211
Valinco Gulf, 184, 185
Vallance, Aylmer, *The Summer King*, 57n.
Vaux, Comte de, 59
Veaux Marins, Grotte des, Calvi, 146
Vecchio gorges, 196, 197
Venaco, 197
Verde, Col de, 210
Vergio, Col de, 203
Vescovato, Consulte de, 56
Vincentello of Istria, 54, 187, 199, 226
Vivario, 170, 196-7, 210
Vizzavona, 90, 194, **195-7**
  Col de, 194
Voltaire, Francois Arouet, *Candide*, 57-8

Walpole, Horace, 57

Zicavo, 210-1
Zonza, 108, 172, 207, **208-10**